Captivating
Cats

Viviann & Keith —
Happy New Year '91

Captivating Cats

Fiona and *Marc* Henrie

Longmeadow Press

This edition is published by
Longmeadow Press
201 High Ridge Road
Stamford, CT 06904

ISBN 0-681-40986-X

Printed in Italy
0 9 8 7 6 5 4 3 2 1

Credits
Editor: Jo Finnis
Designer: Nigel Duffield
Filmsetting by: The Old Mill, England
Color reproduction:
P&W Graphics Pte. Ltd., Singapore

The Author
Fiona Henrie has worked over the last 20 years with
her husband, Marc, photographing animals — cats
in particular — and has accumulated a wealth of
knowledge of their behavior. Fiona has written a
series of pet care books for children and a series of
easy readers, as well as many articles on cats and
reviews of cat books, published in leading animal
magazines in the UK.

The Photographer
Marc Henrie was in great demand by the
Hollywood movie stars to photograph them with
their pets when he worked for the major film
studios early in his career. Later, after he had
returned to England, he specialized in
photographing dogs and cats, setting up his own
business in 1964.

   Marc's work has appeared in numerous pet and
animal books, calendars and magazines both in the
UK and overseas. His many photographic awards
include the Kodak Award for the Best Pet Picture
of the Year (1982) and the Neal Award for the Most
Original Animal Picture (1984).

   Marc is also a judge of non-pedigree cats.

Preface
Joan Moore is an author, journalist and
acknowledged authority on feline matters, both in
the UK and around the world. She is currently
Editor of "Cat World" and "Show World"
magazines in the UK.

Categories

Foreword

*C*ats are notoriously difficult to photograph, but Marc Henrie makes it look easy. I have watched him at work and marvelled at his skill. He has the special knack of knowing the exact moment to act, and has the ability to keep a cat's attention in a way that must be the envy of other photographers. His understanding of the body language of cats is clearly profound. But there is no need to take my word for it. Turn these pages and you will see for yourself that he is, without doubt, the greatest of all feline photographers.

With the accompanying text by his wife, Fiona, this book of superb images will delight all those who have come under the spell of that most fascinating, most contradictory, most graceful of all animals — **Felis sylvestris,** the cat.

Desmond Morris
Oxford, 1990

Preface

Genius is an elusive quality, aspired to by many and achieved by few. 'Captivating Cats' is an accolade to the undoubted genius of Marc Henrie, photographer of animals **par excellence**. Complemented by the talented text of his wife Fiona, this delightful book is also a testimony to a successful husband and wife partnership which is renowned and respected throughout the world of animals.

'Captivating Cats' reflects Marc's passionate involvement with the feline race and this is evident throughout the book via his inherent sense of style and colour and the mystical rapport which exists between himself and his subjects. Whilst some photographs are in natural settings, some incorporate carefully contrived backgrounds which nostalgically suggest another time, another place . . .

The Old Masters are reminiscent in many of the latter and this is subtly implied in the 'Cat and Rat' on pages 88 to 91. The scratches and imperfections of the wooden chair, the frayed and faded foreground fabric provide a homely setting to the main drama of cat intently watching rat scurry across the red-tiled floor. A classic cat and rat situation, as old as time itself and shown here with a clarity and mellow richness of colour recalling the 17th century Dutch school of painting. Reality combined with artistry to create a photographic masterpiece.

Recognizing that often the most downbeat surroundings inherit a rare and special beauty with the presence of a cat, some of these delightful photographs are set in somewhat dour circumstances — a neglected wooden outbuilding, a rain-soaked farmyard. With flair and a strong sense of design, contrasting angles and textured areas lend a rare and compelling **frisson** to these outstanding examples of Marc Henrie's work.

Conversely, a sense of style in the grand manner is blatantly apparent in some of the indoor shots and emphasize to perfection the ability of the cat to adapt to whatever surroundings it happens to be in at the time. These specimens luxuriate on grand pianos, rosewood tables, sumptuous cushions and on the sills of long Edwardian windows, looking out onto leisured lawns. Settings which nonetheless offer glimpses of homely domesticity — a pile of well-loved books, a casually placed copy of a field sports journal. Informal touches to which we can all relate!

The photographic artistry of Marc Henrie is accompanied by Fiona's polished appraisal of the history, care and concept of the cat throughout the ages taking into account the relationship with its sometime friend but often, sadly, its enemy — Man. Many unusual facts are revealed along the way, making 'Captivating Cats' a compulsive read in addition to the veritable visual feast that it is.

Referring to the 'strange rapport' between himself and his feline subjects, Marc feels that they recognize in him a kindred spirit and so, with the perception of their kind, allow him to capture their souls on film. Known to 'talk' to the cats by imitating their voice sounds, Marc finds that this way they respond to him more readily so that **he** is always in control — never the cat!

Accustomed to photographing the Hollywood 'greats' and still with a penchant for those nostalgic, halcyon days of the 'silver screen', Marc is now happy with his feline subjects who, he says, pose with a natural glamour all of their own. To Marc, every cat is a star. He sees a special mood and quality in each and seeks to transpose that quality onto film. Famous for his superb portraits of pedigree cats, Marc feels that every breed requires a different approach — the Birman has a touch of 'wildness' and the Burmese may need a certain 'aggressive approach'. Longhairs, he finds, are slightly aloof.

In this beautifully produced book we see winsome cats, curious cats, inquisitive cats, elegant cats. Cats with kittens, cats with claws, cats in the country, cats in the city. Cats in every mood imaginable. We are transported through the secret, wonderful, magical world of cats where their every expression and mood has been reflected and captured on film.

A tribute to Marc and Fiona Henrie, 'Captivating Cats' is a collector's piece, a work of love and dedication destined to entrance true cat-lovers everywhere.

Joan Moore

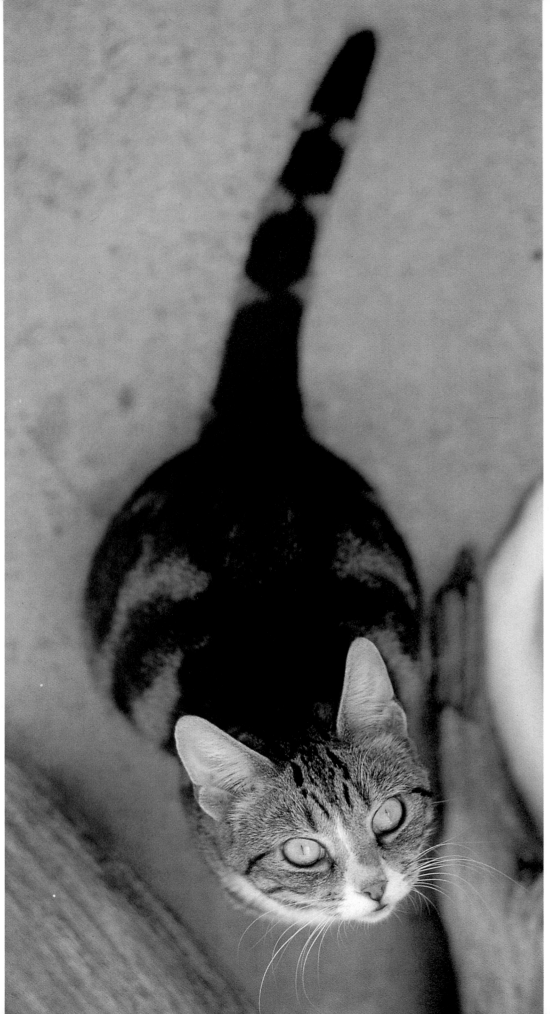

Cat

Fat cats
Thin cats
Scrawny cats and
Dim cats

Brainy cats and
Hairy cats
Smooth ones
Trim ones

Dancing cats
Prancing cats
Progressively advancing cats
Continually entrancing cats
In every kind of play

Fey cats
Gay cats
For ever in the way cats
Night-time or day cats
Always on display

Posing cats
Supposing cats
Pat it on the nose cats
Sink in deepest doze cats
Dreaming their lives away

One eye ever open cats
For favour ever hoping cats
To one side always sloping cats
Which prowl the night away with the

Roof-top and alley cats the
Lolling, dilly-dally cats the
Hill-top and the valley cats
Which are caught up in the fray with the

Fat cats
Thin cats
Scrawny cats and
Dim cats the
Rummage in the bin cats which
Join this quaint array to the

Silken-cushion sinking cats the
Eating and the drinking cats the
Pampered, polished, plushy cats the
Lazy or the rushing cats the
Owners always fussing cats
Polite or quite disgusting cats
Rumbustious or gushing cats and
Those who're led astray from the

Great and noble family of
Feline equanimity
Imperious, mysterious
Amusing or quite serious of
Gargantuan proportions with the
Most inflated notions of their
Own quite great importance in
The scheme of things to come

From the strolling down the Strand
cats to the
Sing with celestial band cats the
Sit on the Left Hand cats when
It comes to Judgement Day will be

A thin cat
A fat cat an
I know what I'm at cat there
Will be no doubt of that, Cat,
Your place awaits your whim

So that when nine lives are over you'll
Be eternally in clover the
Stay at home cat or a rover
Never sink with feet of clay but

Rise a glorious on high cat a
Fearless 'do or die' cat
Gregarious or shy cat
Get up and walk your way. . .

by **Fiona Henrie**

Original Cats

There was a strong wind blowing when it happened. The sand and dust stung his eyes and dulled the well-defined markings of his now matted coat. It was cold, very cold indeed, which sharpened his instincts towards shelter rather than the satisfaction of an aching stomach. It was just then that his nostrils registered the first, faint promise of an odour which he had not encountered before. It was an odour of ... he knew not what, but it suggested food — definitely food, for it made his mouth water. At the same time, he detected the scent of danger, of other creatures, of man himself. He crept closer and closer toward the scent low to the ground, noiseless, pausing occasionally to raise his head into the wind. It was becoming stronger and stronger — he could hardly contain his excitement. Then he saw it! Just ahead a cave mouth yawned a gaping entrance. A dry, sheltered place. Safe? Perhaps not, but the smells which bombarded him made him bold. So he stalked around in a large circle until he was right at the edge of the cave. There he stayed concealed, so he thought, from sight, and waited. The next day he came again and the next, to watch and see all there was to see — still concealed, never showing himself — until one day the woman caught **his** scent and enticed him into the human circle, where he has stayed ever since.

Is this how it happened? Rudyard Kipling in his 'Just So' stories thought so. Perhaps he was right. The origins of the cat remain shrouded in the mists of time — in legend, folklore; in mysticism and religious cults.

According to Frances Simpson, writing in Kensington, London in 1903, an Arabian naturalist tells a fascinating story of the birth of the cat. In Noah's Ark, there was consternation lest the King of the Beasts, the lion, should cause havoc amongst the other animals. So, having prayed to the Almighty, a fever befell the lion, thus restoring peace to the Ark. But, it was thought that, at the other end of the scale, the mouse could do as much damage to provisions and clothing. Again, the Almighty complied. He caused the lion to sneeze and out of his nostrils sprang the cat. Consequently, the mouse became timid and lived in holes from that day forth.

There is no doubt that the lion plays a significant part in the origins of the ancient links between the domestic cat and man. In fact, many of the big cats still in existence have played their part in this connection.

The earliest evidence of humans wearing the skins of animals is at Catalhüyük, the Neolithic site in Anatolia (a part of modern-day Turkey) dated circa 6500 BC, where the fertility goddess is portrayed with leopards. At this hunting shrine, a fairly elaborate cult took place. People riding authentically-marked leopards are depicted. Also, the goddess is shown sitting on a stone throne flanked by two leopards.

At another Neolithic site, at Hacilar (also in Turkey), dated around a thousand years later, a throne made in the shape of a leopard has been found with a woman seated upon it. There are also numerous figurines of women accompanied by leopards and carrying small cats. Perhaps this is the origin of our obsession with the domestic cat — of the cat cult of today!

In Mesopotamia the lion was associated with the goddess of war, Ishtar. In other places the goddess Cybele was associated with the lion — probably the direct descendant of the fertility goddess of Neolithic Anatolia, later to become the 'Great Mother' of the Greeks and Romans.

In Ancient Egypt, where the lion as the symbol of the sun and the bull as the symbol of the moon were worshipped, it was thought that the sun god strangled the moon god at dawn each day. At the temple of the sun god Amon-Re at Heliopolis, the centre of the lion cult, several sacred lions were kept in luxury by attendant priests who bathed them in perfume, burnt incense and fed them choice tit-bits.

The lion was sacred to both the major Indian religions, Buddhism and Hinduism. It was often shown between the feet of Buddha or on a corner of his throne. The Hindu god Vishnu is thought to take on the shape of Narasinha, the man lion, to intimidate a ferocious enemy.

In China, the tiger with the face markings forming the letter 'Van' was thought to be a reincarnation of an important person, usually a king — a belief reitorated in East Africa where former rulers are believed to reincarnate as lions, which makes for a great reluctance to kill them.

In Java and Sumatra, there were 'tiger men' who supposedly turned into tigers, whereas lions and leopards were to the forefront in the secret societies of East and West Africa and their cults in the Old World. In the New World, the primary attraction was to the jaguar and the puma.

In South America the tiger was considered to be an evil spirit — a sorcerer whom it was impossible to fight. Cat cults also played an important part in Amerindian culture.

Guggisberg in his book 'Wild Cats of the World' (1975) considers whether, assuming that man entered the Americas about 30,000 years ago and must have been familiar with the giant Pleistocene tigers of Eastern Siberia, the cat cults derived from Asia or developed independently in the New World in contact with the big cats there but on lines similar to the cat cults of Asia.

Totemistic and animistic beliefs may have originated far back in the Palaeolithic period and may have spread over most of the world long before the leopard cult of Anatolian Catalhüyük.

In Egypt in the second millenium BC the domestic cat first appeared probably as a miniature stand-in for the lion. He came to enjoy a special place in the lives of the people of this time, if not in their culture and their art.

In the grandest of homes, a small reddish-striped cat is seen cavorting beneath the chair of one of two elegant ladies who are playing a board game on the table between them.

A similar cat is shown painted on a mural from a tomb, leaping up to catch a water bird in its mouth while a man in a boat, secreted amongst the reeds, looks on as other birds rise up in fright. This remarkable picture, known as 'Fowling in the Marshes', is upheld as evidence that small, domestic cats were trained to retrieve for man.

The guardian of the most highly revered document of Ancient Egypt, the sacred 'Book of the Dead', is Ra, the cat god. A stylized representation of the cat, Ra is more akin to the Abyssinian breed of cat in existence today than the cat in 'Fowling in the Marshes', or the pet cat of the grand ladies. The latter is closer in appearance to a modern red tabby with its striped coat, or indeed the breed of cat which lays claim to be the 'true' Egyptian Cat — the Egyptian Mau or Oriental Tabby.

The cat was considered sacred to the goddess Bastet who was sometimes shown as a cat-headed human figure seated on her throne with a small cat at each of the four corners, or as the cat itself wearing earrings and necklace.

One of the most ancient representations of the cat is in the necropolis at Thebes,

which contains the tomb of Hana. He is depicted in a statue with Bouhaki, his cat, between his feet.

On a more chilling note, there were times in Egyptian history when it was the custom to throw into the Nile any woman caught in the act of adultery, tied in a sack with a live female cat, the analogy presumably being the supposed promiscuity of the female cat.

On the death of a cat, the ancient Egyptian household went into mourning. The body was embalmed and put into a coffin and transported to the temple of Bast at Bubastis. One of the greatest festivals of the year was the ceremony of entombing these cats. The cats' relatives offered sacrifices and sent their pets off into the next life with presents of food and toys, culminating in a feast for the

participants of food and much wine.

The cats were mummified and wrapped in the conventional style with bands of linen in such a way as to form a woven effect. Many have been found in wooden boxes. Some have the cat's face painted onto the mummy.

It is sad to relate that in the so-called enlightened nineteenth and twentieth centuries when thousands of these cat mummies were excavated, they were used as fertilizer and on the railways.

It is generally accepted that the origins of the British common domestic cat (or 'moggy', as it is widely known) lies with the importation of the Cyprus cat — a plain, greyish brown tabby from that Mediterranean island, brought ashore, perhaps, by Phoenician traders coming to the tin mines of Cornwall. Alternatively, they may have been introduced at a later date via the Roman galleys with Julius Caesar and his legions, carried on board to protect the provisions from vermin.

It is not too difficult to connect the descendants of the Neolithic cats of Hacilar with the Island of Cyprus or with Egypt, where they may have spread via the Mediterranean traders.

It seems that the cult of the cat continued well into the Middle Ages, so perhaps it is not surprising that Christianity turned on any innocent herbalist with a cat, especially a black one, branding her as a witch.

This was a dark period indeed for the cat, regarded as a creature of Satan — a witches' familiar. In parts of Europe it was the custom to kill as many cats as possible. The most awful fate befell cats during Lent in France. The cat population was so seriously depleted to the extent that the course of history itself may well have been influenced by that fact.

The plague was brought to Britain by the rat and spread far and wide, wiping out whole communities. It is possible that the disease might not have been quite so devastating in its effect on the human population had there been more cats — a natural predator — to despatch at least some of the infected rats.

Fortunately today a more liberal attitude is displayed towards this beautiful and affectionate animal by people in general as well as by the Christian church.

Mystical Cats

The elusive quality of the cat, the 'now you see it, now you don't' characteristic, is one of the prime attractions for those people who are convinced of the psychic side of feline life. This creature of the shades and shadows, merging into light and landscape, has appeared and disappeared throughout history as a magical and mysterious link with the cult cats of Catalhüyük (see pages 10 and 12).

*If there is a cat in your household, or has been in the past, you must have noted those occasions when you have been convinced beyond a shadow of a doubt of a low furry object brushing by your legs, passing through the door or leaping through the open window. To find your adored feline fast asleep behind the sofa, having been there all afternoon, does nothing to allay the feeling of disquiet you will experience — indeed, if not a sensation of a stronger nature. **Déjà vu**, perhaps? Or . . .*

Have you ever noticed your cat playing 'Track the Spook?' An unnerving event it is too, especially on the first occasion. To spy your normally well-balanced feline suddenly fix its gaze on a point in mid space, somewhere between the eye and the nearest object, and then follow this elusive 'something' halfway round the room and back, up to the ceiling, down to the floor and eventually out of the door, is an experience which defies explanation.

In countless tales of mystery and imagination, the cat features as prime protagonist; from Edgar Allan Poe's chilling accounts to the horror films starring that master of mortal terror, Vincent Price. They highlight the darker side of feline nature, which has its attractions in some quarters.

Ancient civilizations believed that certain individuals could inhabit the bodies of animals, often the big cats, and the so-called witches of the Middle Ages were thought to change places with the cat which always accompanied them. In this way they were able to venture out and perpetrate their sorcery without being recognized.

Roger Tabor, in his 'Wildlife of the Domestic Cat' (1983), attributes to Baldwin in 'Beware the Cat' the notion that the cat has nine lives because '. . . it is permitted for a witch to take her cat's body nine times . . .'

Because of its apparent psychic qualities, the cat was often the subject of 'hauntings'. When a psychic phenomenon presents itself, the dog will run to hide or howl, in fear, whilst the cat seems to enjoy the situation — at least, it seems to be in sympathy with the 'presence' rather than being alarmed by it.

When we baby-sat for a friend in Belgravia (London) many years ago in an early Georgian terraced house, our cat — a neutered, red long-haired tabby which had been hand-reared and thought that he was a person — amazed us by spending all night on guard outside the baby's bedroom door. We learnt, subsequently, that the house had been reported as being haunted and in consequence was exorcised.

A story is told of a merchant of Messina whose cats became so agitated in one of

the rooms of his house that he opened the door to give them access to the next room, where they scratched the floor in the same manner as in the previous room. This procedure continued all through the house until the front door was reached. Outside the house the cats repeated the scratching but this time on the ground. Intrigued, the merchant followed the cats through the town and out into the countryside far away from the town, where the cats were seen to scratch the ground once more in the same agitated way. It is recorded that an earthquake subsequently took place which destroyed many houses in the town, including that of the merchant!

That a cat should be seen frequenting a churchyard, or that several should be, ought not to be considered unusual. Cats seem to be attracted to dark, solitary places, overhung by the foliage of the cypress tree, shadowed by grey headstones. A cat could spend many a long hour contemplating in such a place.

A Cat's Life

*T*hat delightful little bundle of fun with the soft, appealing eyes; that ultimately winsome creature — a kitten. No-one can deny the attraction of this small, divine animal which, in the fullness of time, will grow up to become a cat. This may seem a most obvious statement to make, but many people are so caught up with the undoubted charm of the young one, that they forget that one day it will become an adult cat and continue, hopefully, into old age, with all the attendant responsibilities and potential problems. If more people could be encouraged to consider this fact carefully — and many are well-intentioned — there might be fewer abandoned cats in the world. Furthermore, if some of the well-intentioned cat owners considered the consequences of an unwanted litter of kittens, then there might be fewer abandoned cats about to give birth, or indeed fewer abandoned kittens.

Consider your cat's life from its own point of view — a complete life of its own: how the kitten develops physically and mentally and becomes an individual with a character all of its own; how it relates to its peers, surroundings and to human beings and other associates, and the special relationship which may develop with an individual. It is also to be hoped that the contact with your feline individual — and, through him, cats in general — will bring a new perspective to the captivating cat.

Kitten Cats

A kitten is the offspring of the cat, born approximately nine weeks, or 63 to 66 days, after conception. It can survive if born up to one week premature or one week after the expected date. There may be only one kitten born, although this is most unusual. Generally there will be any number from three to seven, occasionally more. The largest number of kittens ever recorded in one litter is 15, although the largest number to survive is 11, since four

were still-born. This litter was from a Burmese Siamese mating.

The term 'kitten' is used until the animal becomes sexually mature. This can be as short a period as around 14 weeks with a very precocious female, possibly a Siamese or Oriental type. The usual period of time is around five months, although in the long-haired breeds it will probably be longer — around ten before the female is calling. Male cats should be sexually competent by one year old. It is inadvisable to arrange the mating of a female until she is at least one year old.

Kittens are born with their bodies covered with fur, their eyes and ears closed and unable to stand up on their thin legs. The ears are tiny, folded and flattened against the head. The legs are small in proportion to the body and head. The hind legs move in a kind of paddling motion, enabling the kitten to convey itself towards and away from the teats. The front feet are used with a kind of kneading, up-and-down action against the mother, supposedly to stimulate the flow of milk.

The eyes will open at around one week old; the ears become erect at about three weeks. Two weeks after birth the kitten

should be able to crawl and at about three weeks, be able to stand. By the time the kitten is six weeks old it should be strong, lively and able to groom itself.

By this time the kitten will be inquisitive and anxious to explore as much of its world as possible — and beyond. By the time the kittens are fully weaned they will be ready to go to their new homes, if necessary, and find completely new surroundings to explore.

It would be misleading to address the prospective cat owner, since no-one ever actually 'owns' a cat. I think it would be true to say that the cat has a will of its own. Although it may live with you, sleep with you, accept food from you, play with you, talk to you and love you, being your shadow and ever-loving slave, it will still maintain an essential spirit of independence. In other words, it will still not belong to you. A dog, on the other hand, gives himself to you body and soul: "I will wag my tail for you forever!"

So, it is important for the prospective cat 'guardian' (for want of a better word) to decide what kind of cat he or she wishes to share his or her life. Are you attracted to an elegant Oriental or Siamese? — then

be prepared for 'vocals' at any or all times; or the dog-like Burmese, sleek and intelligent; alternatively, one of the full-coated Persians — a puff ball of beauty — if you have hours to spare, loads of patience and a penchant for brushing and combing.

The Abyssinian is perhaps the breed of pedigree cat most like the non-pedigree or domestic cat — the best of both worlds! But if your leaning towards a pedigree is equivocal, just think 'cat'.

All kittens should be full of fun and eager to play, although since they are young creatures they will tire after a period of time, depending on their age, and will need to rest. A kitten which sits about and looks miserable should be investigated. Seek expert advice.

Be sure to register your pet with a local veterinarian and ask for advice on vaccinations and health care.

Kittens, like children, need to be watched carefully to make sure they are not recklessly mischievous. There are all kinds of dangers awaiting them in the

home and the garden. At first it might be best to restrict your charge to one room — most people find the kitchen is best, with serviceable flooring and the absence of the more precious and vulnerable furniture, which could be seriously damaged by sharp little claws on a scratching spree. All that is necessary for a kitten is a place of its own which will not be disturbed. A dry cardboard box will suffice, with some warm bedding in the bottom; its own food dish and water bowl, kept out of the way and in the same place all the time so that they can be easily located by the new puss. Also, the all-important litter or toilet tray, kept away from the bed and food bowls.

When it comes to the great outdoors, climbing is one of the activities kittens like best. They are generally confident and competent — at least, going up is easy; not so coming back down again.

At about six to eight weeks, the proportions of the kitten's body and legs will begin to alter — the body will slim and lengthen and the legs will also become longer. The head will lengthen and alter in proportion so that the ears do not seem quite so large. The antics may continue for some time, but the endearing kitten ways will come to an end. But in most cats there remains throughout their lives a tiny spark of youth which shows itself from time to time in the odd mad moment — which indicates quite clearly that, at any age, your cat can still be a 'kitten cat'.

Tom Cats

'Tom cat' is the term used to designate the male cat. How it came to be called the tom has been impossible to discover. It is applied to some other animals, but the tom cat is the most well-known. Tom was a kind of primitive sluice used in the US, provided with a strainer for catching large stones. In ship-building, a tom is a small shore or brace placed between two frames. Surely that can have no connection. 'Tum' is a sound made by a musical string of little resonance, usually repeated as in the 'tum tum' of the banjo. Could there be a connection here? Tum in Egyptian mythology was a form of the sun god, representing the close of the day, as Horos did its beginning. Are we getting nearer? Or perhaps 'tom' is linked with the word 'tumble' — to perform acrobatic feats. Cats are certainly exceedingly good at that. The word 'tam', a version of 'tom', leads us to 'tamable' — that which may be tamed; susceptible to being made docile, domesticated or civilized. Could the simplest explanation be the right one? Have we simply a tamed cat, a tam cat, a tom cat?

If this is the correct explanation of the term 'tom cat', then why should it apply only to the male? Perhaps at one time it applied to both male and female, but when 'tom' came into exclusive use it was connected with the male name, Thomas, therefore excluding the female.

The tom cat, in the modern use of the term, is the male, domesticated cat; entire, un-neutered (un-altered — US). He becomes sexually mature up to 12 months of age. In pedigree cats the Orientals are more sexually precocious, some of which are mature from five months onwards. The Persian and other long-haired varieties tend to mature later, although the average for all cats is around seven months.

Tom cats mark the boundaries of their territory in various ways — one of which is by spraying urine on a tree, wall or rock. This is done in a completely different fashion to the normal passing of urine. The cat will stand with its hind quarters facing the object to be marked and eject a fine spray in a forceful manner. This has a most pungent, acrid odour, which is

exceedingly difficult to eliminate, as you will know if you have ever been the unfortunate recipient of a full tom cat spray in your home. A female cat will spray too, on occasions, but this is thought to be a way of informing the male cats in the area that she is in season. Neutered cats spray too, but this is often considered to be abnormal behaviour, although it may be part of the territory-making exercise. In the spring time when cats are active, if the scent of tom cats is prevalent around the exterior of a house, a neutered tom inside the house may be induced to spray on the nearest interior points, by a door or window. It carries an unpleasant odour, but fortunately it does not have the full force of the entire tom.

The estimated territory of the male forest wild cat (**Felis sylvestris sylvestris** and related subspecies, **caucasia, grampia** etc) covers a well-defined area of about 128 acres (52 hectares) in the Carpathian forests, but this varies according to local conditions. The male defends its territory against other toms but does not hesitate to pass far beyond its boundaries when forced to do so by shortage of food or to find a female at mating time. Within its home range, each animal has several dens or resting places and a series of well-used tracks and a number of trees which it stands up against to scratch on the bark. This gesture is usually referred to as 'sharpening the claws', although it may also be a form of territory marking.

The domestic cat behaves in a similar way and can often be seen scratching the bark of a tree. The side of the face and neck are often used to 'mark' a place, another animal or even a person. There are glands in parts of the body which deposit a scent on the area rubbed by the cat. Next time puss winds himself around your legs in that affectionate way we all know and rubs his face and neck against you, he is actually stating: "You are mine, you are now my property."

Anyone who has ever been unable to sleep due to rooftop or garden cats courting a female can testify to the noise level of the caterwauling! Tom cats have been known to leave home and be gone for days on the trail of a calling female in the vicinity. It is said that the sex urge is the

strongest driving force there is — nature's way of preserving the species.

Within the realms of cat breeding, a full tom who has proved himself capable of siring young and has distinguished himself in the show world (winning prizes and perhaps becoming a champion) is in great demand as a stud cat.

Because of the anti-social nature of his territorial activities already mentioned, it is not usual to keep a stud cat in the home, but house him in special quarters of his own outside.

Loneliness is a problem with the stud cat, who may be on his own, confined to his quarters between visiting queens. Some owners overcome this by housing a neutered animal with him for company.

The tom cat is a solitary animal, we are told, only coming together with a female for the purposes of mating. This may be so in the wild or in rural areas where there is plenty of room for each cat to have a wide territory of its own, but in the more confined conditions of urban and sub-urban life, there seem to be more cats at large than ever before. In cities and towns where cats are plentiful and free-ranging and where gardens and open spaces are quite small, some cats have taken to

leaving faeces on the surface of the ground rather than burying them, which is their natural habit. This may be considered another form of territory marking, perhaps even a protest against overcrowding.

In households where there are several, if not many, cats they generally seem to sort themselves out into some kind of pecking order, with the 'boss' cat usually being an un-neutered male, although this is not always so. In some situations it seems as though the sociable kitten habits of sharing a bed have prevailed. In a centrally-heated home, warmth could not be said to be the reason for this. Where there are kittens around it has been known not only for the other female adults to take a hand (paw!) in the up-bringing of the young, but the neutered males and sometimes the tom, too. In the US, I met a Maine Coon family of cats in Massachusetts where father took more interest in washing the kittens than the mother. Apparently he did not spray and was therefore allowed to stay in the house.

Mother Cats

"Who is 'she' — the cat's mother?" How often have we heard adults chiding children in this way — a throwback to a bygone time when the female cat was referred to as the 'she' cat. The cat's mother is generally a good one, in that she is caring and conscientious. There are rare exceptions, when the mother cat refuses to feed the kittens, to wash them or protect them. This can indicate a health problem with the kittens.

When the queen is in oestrus, that is the period of time when she will accept a male, she can become most vociferous, making awful howling noises which can sound quite agonizing. One might be tempted into thinking that she is in pain, but this is not so. She will also display some apparently affectionate behaviour — rolling on the ground, rubbing herself against legs and asking for attention. She might also spray — not so affectionate, you might be forgiven for thinking. Should your cat be outside, this spraying will serve to attract any, and perhaps all, the entire tom cats in the area — her way of passing on the information, should they have failed to hear the vocalizing! This

behaviour may begin in the period of time just prior to oestrus, known as pro-oestrus. A sign that your queen may be about to come into heat is the nipples becoming pinker. Cat breeders refer to this as 'pinking up'.

Un-neutered (entire or un-altered — US) females allowed to roam freely, feral cats and any pedigree queen who has managed to escape the fold, which she will try to do with remarkable persistence, will almost certainly get mated by one if not several of the local tom cats, becoming pregnant (or in kitten) as a consequence. The locality would have to be one of extreme isolation for there not to be at least one entire tom cat within striking distance.

A queen may be mated many times during oestrus by several suitors. This is known as super fecundity. In the resulting litter each kitten many have been fathered by a different tom, hence the enormous variety of kittens which can appear in any one litter. This phenomenon is utilized by breeders of cats in controlled conditions. It is usual for the queen who is in oestrus, or is about to be, to visit the tom cat on his premises. She will be introduced to him gradually to ensure that he will accept her. If this proves to be the case, he will have the opportunity to mate her more than

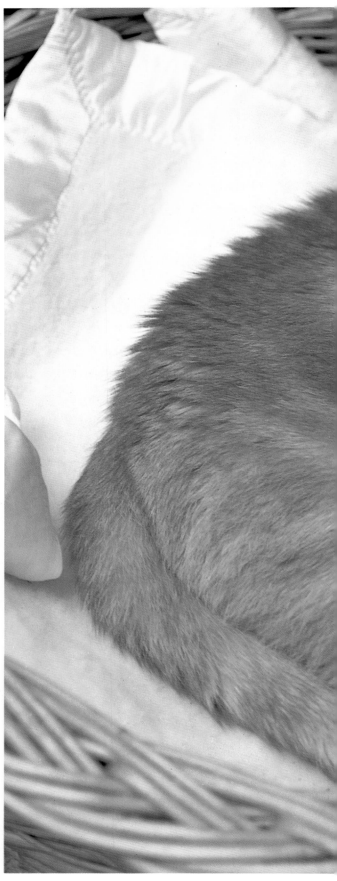

once, to increase the likelihood of pregnancy and the size of the litter.

Sometimes a queen will have a second period of oestrus after the first is over. If she is mated again while pregnant the resulting kittens will be proportionately younger than the first. It is possible for this second litter to develop and be born at the same time as the first litter, when they will probably be still-born, although alternatively they may continue to develop in the uterus and born to term.

The queen's appearance does not alter much during the first three weeks or so of pregnancy but by around five weeks it is possible for a veterinarian to detect the number of kittens by abdominal palpation. It is not a good idea for an inexperienced person to try this since damage to the kittens may occur. Latterly, it will be possible to see first a slight then a much greater bulging of her sides.

About a week or so before the kittens are due, the queen will show signs of being restless and start looking for what she considers is a suitable place to give birth to her litter. It will no doubt be a highly unsuitable place from any point of view except that of the pregnant queen, for

instance at the back of a warm cupboard or the middle of a favourite bed! A special kitten box should be provided, to which the queen should be encouraged to become accustomed.

Feral cats will have their kittens wherever they can find suitable accommodation in the location in which they find themselves. Both urban and rural ferals tend to live in colonies or groups, some quite large in numbers of cats, where they have been left to breed indiscriminately: the corner of an outhouse or deserted farm building in a rural situation or in the cellars of derelict buildings, beneath hospitals or office blocks in towns and cities. Some of these queens will be domestic cats that have turned to 'the wild' and others will be feral born, maybe several generations on.

If any cat — domestic, wild or feral — is not happy for any reason with the site she has selected for the birth of her kittens, she will change the location forthwith. Even after the kittens are born, the mother cat will systematically move each kitten one at a time, in her mouth, and relocate her family elsewhere, if not entirely satisfied. Mother cats have been known to move their litters several times, especially if disturbed.

The conscientious mother will feed her kittens exclusively for about three weeks, after which they can take experimental quantities of cats' milk substitute, baby cereal, baby foods or branded, specially-prepared kitten food until they are completely weaned. A feral litter will have to rely on mother's skill as a huntress, or the administrations of friendly feeders.

Until they are able to wash themselves, the queen will lick them all over to clean and stimulate them.

Old Cats

Cats are highly skilled at disguising the fact that they are feeling less than well. They have what we would call a high pain threshold. In fact, their bodies release a chemical which masks the pain or discomfort. Consequently, a cat can be quite ill before any outward signs are visible.

The attentive owner may be able to detect the early-warning signs of a deterioration in well-being throughout their cat's life simply by noticing changes in its behaviour. Any change, however small, can be significant, since cats are such great creatures of habit. However, when the cat moves into old age, there are additional signs of ill-health for the caring owner to look out for.

Some cats show early signs of growing old, while others live to a ripe old age in cat terms still behaving like kitten-cats. What is 'a ripe old age' for a cat? They are reputed to have nine lives; just how long is their life expectancy? An eight month-old kitten could be said to be the equivalent of a child of ten. A one year-old adolescent cat can be likened to a human teenager of 15. A four year-old cat is in its early middle age – its human counterpart would be 40 years of age, when maybe we can expect life to begin? The Bible's expectancy of a fulfilled life-span of three score years and ten (70) would correspond to a cat of 15 years of age, and the few human stalwarts of our time who have reached the incredible age of 90 could call in their feline counterparts at 20. Although very few cats attain the age of 30, we know of one which reached the age

of 29, so by the calculation here employed she was 120 years-old in human terms.

The elderly cat may not be as efficient at grooming out any dead hairs as it was in the past, resulting in a dull, dry coat with matted areas, if no human aid is given. So extra grooming is required.

As with elderly people, the elderly cat sometimes needs a change in diet, but since cats tend to only like the kind of food they are used to eating, effecting the change could prove to be a problem. It would be a good idea to discuss this with your veterinarian and ask their advice before any changes in diet are made.

There are some diseases to which elderly cats are particularly prone, which can be treated if discovered in time. Several of these ailments share a common symptom: an increase in thirst. Therefore, if your cat is drinking more water than usual, arrange

a veterinary examination immediately. In any event, always provide plenty of fresh drinking water.

Your elderly cat deserves the very best quality of life, having given life-long companionship. So, pander to him a little. Provide an extra warm bed — perhaps a bean bag instead of a basket or a plastic bed. If your cat is very elderly or frail, a heated pad, especially in very cold weather, will be much appreciated. It is not a good idea to let your cat stay outside for too long in very cold weather.

When the sad moment of parting approaches, you hope it will be peaceful, painless and natural, but this is not always possible. There may come a time when **you** will have to decide if the quality of your cat's life is satsifactory. No-one wants to think about euthanasia, but we must consider ourselves fortunate to have the means to end suffering and pain, to be able to permit our pets to depart this life with dignity.

Cat Habits

*T*he cat is a creature of habit, as anyone who has had the privilege of sharing their life with one or more of these fascinating, infuriating and beguiling creatures will be able to tell you. However, the cat is also a creature of paradox. Just when you think you know its every thought and action, it confounds you with an uncharacteristic act. What is more, this behaviour will, in all likelihood, be the exact opposite in nature to your feline's customary routine.

Our gentle puss is a carnivorous (meat-eating) mammal which will hunt and kill its prey, in the same way as the large members of the cat family, (Felidae). The domestic cat, while able and willing to perform this natural role of hunter, still presumes the provision of food, and that of only the best quality, the choicest cuts.

The cat's curiosity is outstripped only by cunning intelligence and the ability to doze at any time or in any place, no matter how unlikely a spot or uncomfortable a position.

When it comes to stealth and agility, there is no creature able to challenge the cat.

A complicated system of communication is used within the feline world, from one cat to another using sound, scent and body language. This is a network into which you may tune if you know, or are willing to learn, the signals.

Once you have formed the habit of sharing your life with a cat, you will never wish to be broken of it.

Hunting and Feeding

*T*he cat's instinct for hunting is very strong indeed. Even when well fed with a regular and as near perfect diet as possible, this instinct is still so strong that a domestic cat will hunt and catch small birds, voles and mice.

A Siamese cat recently displayed such a strong hunting instinct that it would only eat if the food bowl was hidden in a different place each day so that the cat had to 'hunt' for it.

The domestic cat hunts in a similar way to the wild cat. It glides noiselessly along, close to the ground using eyes, ears and nose. It then pounces on its prey. Many cat owners are disturbed by their pets' treatment of its captive prey — worrying or playing with the creature.

The hunting, catching instinct is transferred to a simulated situation, both with kittens and adult cats, using a 'toy' mouse, a ball of paper or whatever comes to paw! Kittens practise the procedure in

this way even in the wild, with a leaf or a small piece of bark.

I once saw a farm cat bring a small rabbit which she had caught back to the farmhouse, whereupon she scratched at the window until it was opened. She presented her prey to the occupants of the room for them to admire her hunting prowess, and then proceeded to devour the creature in its entirety. Meanwhile, her son, who was too lazy to hunt, looked on.

All members of the cat family are carnivorous. In addition, they do ingest some vegetable matter, but this is most likely to come from the stomach contents of their prey. Domestic cats are often seen eating grass, which they need to maintain good health. Cats which are kept entirely indoors need to have some growing grass provided for them. Most pet stores or suppliers sell small pots of grass to grow indoors by a window. Cats (and dogs, too) seem to use grass as an emetic. A cat will often be seen eating grass only to regurgitate it along with a fur ball.

The cat's long, curved claws are an aid to catching and killing prey and also for defending itself in a fight. These claws are retractile, which means that they can be drawn back between the pads to prevent them rubbing on the ground and becoming blunt. Cats' feet are digitigrade, which means that they walk on their toes. They have five toes on the fore feet, four on the front of the foot which touch the ground and one (the thumb or **pollex**) which does not touch the ground. The latter is sometimes known as a dew claw. On the hind feet there are four toes with

Mrs M Chance in her delightful book published in 1898, which she illustrated with her own most expressive pencil drawings, tells of a physician in Calcutta who had a servant whose express task it was to make curry for his 20 cats.

In 1862, a fascinating book was published in London — a tome entitled 'The Management of Household Pets'. Quoted in this book is an anecdote about a Mr Wood who, while on a visit to Paris, chanced to share a table at a pavement café with an Angola (**sic**) — a cat with long fur, pointed ears and a brush tail. Presumably this was an Angora. The cat looked at him with such appeal that he felt obliged to share an almond biscuit with the poor creature. He gave the cat a second biscuit, then a third. Amused, he ordered a whole plateful for the cat, which consumed the lot. He then left the café, not wishing to continue the experiment!

claws; the big toe (**hallux**) is missing. The soft pads on the underside of the feet aid noiseless hunting.

The cat has a most unusual tongue in that its surface is entirely covered with minute horny barbs (**papillae**), which give rise to the expression that the cat has a tongue like sandpaper. These barbs give a rasping effect on contact which makes it possible for the cat to lick all the meat from a bone, or the hair from an animal skin. It is also a great help in grooming its own fur.

In AD 1260, there was a sultan living in Egypt who was exceedingly fond of cats. El-Daher-Beybars was so entranced by them that he bequeathed his garden to them, Gheyt-el-Quottah meaning 'The Cats' Orchard', near his mosque just outside Cairo, making provision for the cats to be fed always.

Gautier's cat, Eponine, was fed at the table along with the human diners and is reputed to have stayed throughout the meal, eating each course in turn — a privilege bestowed upon the cat in recognition of her extreme intelligence.

That famous man of letters, Dr Johnson, went out himself to purchase oysters for his cat, named Hodge, in case the servants, having to take such particular trouble for a cat, should take a dislike to the creature.

Cat Nap

Definition: Sleep is a state of repose, or quiescence, occurring periodically in man and animals, characterized by complete or partial unconciousness.

'To sleep, perchance to dream . . .'

Sleep! Cats do it so well — and they do such a lot of it! They look so relaxed and at ease with themselves and their surroundings that I am sure we can gain in some way from their supreme repose simply by observing it. Relaxation is such a rare commodity in our age of rush, hustle and bustle, pressure and tension. To be able to relax like a cat is a most desirable aspiration for those living under the strain of modern urban and international life. We would do well to try to emulate the cat in this respect.

It is not quite true to say that the cat is a nocturnal creature. It could be called semi-nocturnal, in that it has periods of activity at twilight and just before dawn when it does its hunting. It was a traditional final chore of the day, before

retiring, to 'put the cat out', before the advent of the cat door or flap. It is true that their eyes are adapted for night hunting, for good observation in low-light conditions.

A cat which goes out to hunt in the evening and is then shut out until morning has no alternative other than to stay out all night. Those cats lucky enough to have been furnished with a bolt hole, a cat door, a route of their own to the outside world, will often return to sleep, not stirring until a pre-dawn foray seems to be the order of the day. This does not mean that these cats will not wish to sleep during the day. Quite the contrary, in fact. They might have several periods of sleep of varying kinds, plus a few cat naps, as well as a good deal of just sitting about looking rather dozy.

Just where your cat will choose to sleep is quite another matter, but still one for serious consideration. Just where? The warmest spot, the most comfortable, a good vantage point, a cosy nest, a quiet corner? In fact, you can be sure it will be anywhere except the splendid cat bed which you have acquired at some trouble

and expense. Leave any odd basket or cardboard box lying around and see how quickly these lowly containers become puss's favourite napping place.

Stretched out on the window sill, soaking up as much of the sun as possible before it moves around — this site also provides a splendid vantage point from which to survey the world, as well as being an excellent sitting-about place.

There is no doubt that cats are attracted to warmth, particularly when it comes to finding a place to sleep or even just to doze. The body temperature drops during sleep, so a warm site will compensate for this. A heated pad placed in the cat's bed will greatly improve its attractiveness as a sleeping place.

The cat spends approximately two-thirds of its life asleep and sleeps twice as much as other animals. No one seems to know quite why this is. Just how much sleep a cat will take in a day varies considerably. Firstly, it will vary from cat to cat. Weather conditions come into play too, the rise and fall in temperature and whether the cat has eaten recently. The age of the cat is an

additional factor. Kittens will take more sleep than a healthy adult cat, as will the elderly and those individuals who may be weak or suffering from ill-health.

When the cat first falls asleep there will be a period of relatively light sleep which will last for a short time. The cat will then lapse into a very deep sleep, which can last a considerable period of time, followed by another period of light sleep. During the shallow-sleep periods it may be possible to wake the cat easily.

Some people, it is said, can sleep on a clothes line. The feline equivalent can find places even more bizarre. The top of a ladder is a great favourite; on a radiator is another special place, although there seems precious little space for a cat to perch comfortably. One cat we know insists on sleeping sitting up with its head and neck resting against a vertical support.

Whether the cat you come upon taking a siesta is deeply asleep, in a shallow sleep, simply dozing, or making a very good

pretence of any one of those states, you can ascertain to some extent by the position of the cat's body.

The cat curled up in a circle, or very nearly, with the front paws and tail tip up to the nose, is in a deep sleep. Lying on its side or crouched **lion couchant** style with the head slightly down indicates an intermediate stage. However, lying on its side, legs stretched out with as much of its body surface area in contact with a cold floor as possible, is a cat's way of keeping as cool as it can be in hot weather. If this pose is discovered with the participant lying between two doors in a current of air, then this would confirm it. The head level or right down on the paws is the typical pose of the dozing cat. The eyes may be closed, almost closed or one eye slightly

open. Alternatively, it could be just pretending to be asleep?

Cats are particularly fond of squeezing themselves into such small places that one would think it impossible for them to fit into them, if it was not for the evidence of one's own eyes. They are exceptionally good at contorting their lithe bodies, winding themselves up into a tight ball or stretching out until they appear long and flat, or twisting backwards and forwards, round curves and bends until one might imagine them to be made of elastic. The fact that they can sleep in these extraordinary positions is even more astonishing: in the gap between a cupboard and a wall, at the head of the bed between the stored suitcases and the wall, in the shopping basket, in a tiny drawer, under a low chair. Some cats will even climb up into the underside of a car (a place to be discouraged at all costs); even under the bonnet is not unusual. On top of the car or on the bonnet are favourites, especially after the car has been in motion, while the bonnet is still warm. Of

course the exterior of the car becomes quite warm if left in the sun, so that provides an additional attraction.

The adult cat makes quite a performance out of settling down to sleep. The preliminaries are somewhat theatrical the selection of a suitable spot, the stretch, the circling round and round, then unwinding to sit or coiling into a ball — whatever has been decided.

Kittens on the other hand, like human babies, just drop. They fall asleep in an instant, right before your eyes. A young kitten was once being photographed at about four or five weeks of age. It was sitting crouched like a miniature lion, quite alert and bright. In the next instant, its little head fell forward onto its front paws. After a short nap of about ten minutes, it was running about.

Before relaxing and after sleep as it rises to move off, the cat will stretch first the forelegs, following through the spine and the hind legs. A wonderful, elegant stretch. No wonder cats stay so fit, active and relaxed!

Curiosity
Killed the . . .

*C*uriosity killed the cat! Quite how this expression originated is somewhat obscure, but it does seem to have been well illustrated by the eighteenth century English poet, Thomas Gray, in his 'Ode on the Death of a Favourite Cat, Drowned in a Tub of Gold Fishes'.

Goldfish bowls tend to be frowned upon today as being too small to house fish satisfactorily — they offer too small a water surface area to absorb sufficient oxygen. The most splendid tanks of incredible proportions can be purchased today, together with strikingly-coloured, sparkling fish, waving plants and panoramic backgrounds — better than television for the entertainment of the discerning feline. Fortunately these tanks come with suitable covers to thwart such fishing expeditions as might have been planned but, in any event, it is not too splendid an idea to allow puss access to the room where the fish reside, not so much for the cat's safety as for the peace of mind of the aquatic inhabitants.

Cats are most certainly curious but, at the same time, careful and cautious, particularly when adult — except of course for the odd, mad creature which thinks it is a hurricane or whirling dervish.

Safety in the home is worth considering just as carefully for your feline as for children — perhaps even more so since cats are so much more agile and can obtain heights that children only dream of reaching. How many impish young children would give their last sweet or favourite plaything to be able to shin up the curtains or view the world from the top of the wardrobe! Puss can.

The boiling saucepan on the stove or hob, uncovered with handle protruding over the floor — how tempting for the adolescent puss. How easy it would be to leap from the floor to catch that tail in the air, poised so temptingly and so still! The consequences do not bear thinking about. That live electric flex snaking its way across the floor is tempting, too. A quick tweak with a paw — the creature moved! — then jump in for the kill. Got it! What

a good chew this makes!!!!! The flex which hangs down from the table lamp — another lovely but potentially deadly toy. Trailing plants are especially attractive to cats. Kittens particularly love to chew the leaves and have been known to rapidly defoliate an entire plant. Apart from the wanton destruction, some house plants are poisonous to cats, as are certain garden plants, trees and bulbs.

Open cupboard doors present an exciting temptation, something that the curious, fun-seeking kitten, or even adult cat must investigate. What joys can be found in that dark, sweet-smelling place? It could be a warm and comfortable haven, ideal for that siesta after lunch if it should happen to be the airing cupboard or blanket drawer.

Or it could be a hell-hole of horrors, a proverbial Pandora's Box — if it should happen to be the cupboard under the sink, with the bleach bottle unscrewed or the dry cleaning fluid ready to fall.

As a kitten there is so much to discover in the big, wide world that curiosity is a huge asset. After the home environment has been thoroughly examined from end to end, the great outdoors is waiting with its myriad of scents, sounds and sensations. Whatever time of year it may be there will always be something to explore. The feel of fresh, springy grass under paw, the brush of a flower petal and all the wonderful, new 'green' smells associated with spring time. Perhaps a small mouse or a tiny vole passed this way not long ago. Whatever it was, it is certainly whisker-twitching!

When our exertions are over, what more decadent way to relax than to stretch out on a rooftop, soak up the sunshine and contemplate life's complexities reflected in a raindrop suspended on a spider's web . . .

Agility

*T*hat the cat is a creature of great agility, capable of performing tremendous feats of acrobatic prowess, cannot be denied.

From early kittenhood, once the basic steps have been mastered, one of the first inclinations in a young cat is to climb — anything, anywhere. From chair legs to trouser legs, kittens are not to be deterred!

Most cats are climbers; some are ecstatic climbers and a few are excessively so. The latter are generally of Oriental blood, the Orientals themselves, the Siamese and Burmese, the Devon and Cornish Rexes and not forgetting quite a number of those masters of the feline race, the household non-pedigree or 'moggy'.

It is the cat's particular anatomy which gears it for such nimble operations. With its lithe, muscular, deep-chested body, relatively short limbs and long tail, it is primed for power and balance.

The forelegs are capable of rotatory motion, making easy a change of direction when in flight and making it possible for the cat to grip an object large or small, say a tiny creature or perhaps the trunk of a tree or an adversary. The hind legs provide motive power for jumping and leaping which the cat executes with ease and can, in fact, make an almost vertical take-off from a standing start.

To climb the willow tree on a fresh, late spring day, with the blue sky peeping through sun-spangled leaves, even though there may not be a bird in sight, is an exercise sufficient to warm the heart of any feline.

It is with breathless admiration that we view the balletic excesses of the fabulous feline; the natural fluidity of line and

movement which any dancer would envy. They progress without any kind of effort, so it seems, almost as though moving through water. But the tension is in evidence which reflects the underlying effort involved in portraying such a spectacle of ease.

Should there ever, heaven forbid it, be an accident, that such an acrobat should fall, then the cat's automatic rectifying sequence will be called into operation whereby its body will pass through an angle of 180 degrees to land safely upon its sure feet.

The ability to move in almost any plane and perform at almost any angle makes the cat one of the most supple creatures alive. It can insinuate its lithe body through the narrowest of openings and almost pour out from a hole like the contents of a jug of cream.

How often have we marvelled at the view from our window of the local cats negotiating the narrow fences and trellises which separate and decorate our gardens and parks. They nonchalantly step along a narrow wall or ledge, impossibly narrow to carry a creature of the cat's size one would think, but still they defy our pessimism and perform with breathtaking skill.

The narrowness of the cat's body and the fact that its fore limbs are positioned so close together, coupled with the action of the feet, makes this athletic display an everyday experience. The cat walks in a straight line, placing one paw in front of the other. Combined with the balancing power of the tail, this enables the cat to complete difficult manoeuvres with consummate ease.

Even swinging from the rafters or traversing the beams high up in the roof — like a feline form of Harold Lloyd — is as simple for our feline protagonist as it is for us to negotiate a footpath or to cross a road. It is even possible for our intrepid puss not only to walk along these narrow boundaries but, should the inclination take him, to sit, perched like a fat broody hen, surveying the world below from a precarious perch.

Catastrophe!

_S_ome people are more accident-prone
that others. In fact, certain individuals
cannot move in any direction without
causing unintentional disruption.

Similarly, in the cat world there are
some individuals more inclined to have
accidents than others; that are more likely
to knock over obstacles.

Consider, for example, the case of a
large pedigree, long-haired cat, stocky and
full-coated. One would imagine, judging
by appearances, that this cat could be
nothing but clumsy, knocking ornaments
flying at every turn in its attempt to
negotiate a crowded mantelpiece. But this
is not so; quite the contrary in fact.

Our elegant, dainty, short-haired cat, an
Oriental, Siamese, or any cat with oriental
blood; one would imagine these cats to be
the masters of the assault course, careful
and nimble in the extreme. In practice,
they will dumbfound you with their
excitement and lack of care and will be
more than likely to send objects crashing
to the floor. Of course, there will always
be the few exceptions to the rule.

Communicating

Cats communicate with their own kind, with other creatures and with human beings in domestic situations. In the wild it is unlikely that they form any kind of lasting relationships with other animals, which of course they are otherwise able to do with man's help (or interference!) They communicate with sound, scent, touch and movement, ie body language. With a few clues to guide you, it will not take long for you to reach an understanding of what the various sounds and signs mean, which in turn will promote a deeper understanding of the whole basis of feline life in general.

The way a cat looks or holds its ears or its tail, or even the position of its body, can be a tell-tale sign of how it is feeling or reacting to a particular situation or event. It can even give us an indication of what the cat is about to do next.

The first sense to develop in a kitten is its sense of smell, even while it is still in the nest with eyes and ears closed and only able to move by paddling its way along. Kittens generally go back to the same nipple to suckle and find this one by their own body scent which they have previously left there. If they should happen to venture beyond the environs of the nest, they are able to find their way back to it by employing their sense of smell.

After the eyes and ears are operational and movement is beginning to be co-ordinated, the kitten has all the equipment it needs to function in the feline world. Of course it has a lot to learn and even more to acquire if it is to function happily and in a balanced way in the far more complex sphere of human existence.

In the nest, the kittens learn to react to their peers and to their mother. She has a complex series of sounds which she uses to speak to them, from an almost constant purring to a series of mews and purrs to encourage or admonish them. They will be well used to the feel of her tongue on their bodies by the time they are old enough to groom themselves, from the first moments after birth when she will have licked them dry of the amniotic fluid and nosed them towards a nipple to suckle. In due course, she will hold down a squirming kitten

with a firm paw to wash it, or evade a potentially dangerous situation by carrying the kitten away in her mouth. The sensation of the queen's mouth on the back of the kitten's neck imparts a feeling of discipline: "Mother means what she says and no nonsense" and she may pick up an errant kitten in this way and shake it. The kittens become used to the sounds the queen makes and react accordingly. Equally, it is thought that the mother recognizes each kitten's distress call and therefore can account for each one.

Kittens learn firstly how to react to each other and then to any other animals that there may be in the household, including human beings. If a kitten is going to be a good pet it is important that it is handled frequently while quite young, and exposed to the normal household sounds so that it can become accustomed to them. All this is vital for the kitten's development so that it can grow up to become a well-adjusted cat.

Play amongst kittens and 'sole' play are the building blocks of the adult cat's social behaviour and hunting skills. What enjoyable lessons!

Some cats use sound very minimally and some are exceedingly vocal. Those with the most to say for themselves are usually the Siamese, some of which talk incessantly with that characteristic deep-throated sound quite unlike the voice of any other cat.

Kittens mew when in distress and when hungry, but as they grow their vocabulary grows accordingly.

The cat's purr is, like much about this elusive creature, an enigma. No-one can say for certain how the sound is made or indeed why. The standard theory is that it is produced by the 'false voice box', which comprises two folds of membrane situated behind the real vocal chords in the larynx. More recently, there have been suggestions that it is caused by the vibrations of turbulence in the bloodstream which echo

in the sinus cavities of the skull. Whatever the cause, that continuous vibratory sound is the one associated with the happiness and well-being of a contented cat. It has also been suggested that some cats purr when in pain or discomfort.

"A cat may look at a king" or at another cat; even the way they look at each other has a meaningful construction waiting to be applied. Looking in a gentle way, each cat with face and whiskers relaxed, the pupils of the eyes normal for the light available at the time and both with erect ears, and you have two happy cats greeting each other.

Two cats looking at each other, staring or glaring, and you are usually witnessing the signal for a confrontation!

Generally, one cat will be the aggressor and one on the defensive. Which is which can be determined by posture. An angry cat has a tensed face — the pupils of the eyes will be constricted to mere slits. The ears will be kept erect but will be swivelled backwards in characteristic fashion and the whisker pads blown up to send the whiskers bristling forward. When a cat is frightened it opens its eyes very wide indeed, lays its ears flat on top of the head pointing outwards and flattens its whiskers to follow suit. A cat in ecstasy shows a relaxed face and ears, whiskers in the normal position but the eyes will be half closed.

When two cats meet and favour each other with a malevolent stare, that is usually regarded as a signal for confrontation. One cat will start the ball rolling, as it were, by becoming the aggressive party, while the other assumes the defensive role.

The aggressor will sniff the area at the base of the other's tail whilst growling with ears erect and pupils constricted. The tail will be swishing low to the ground and close to the body. The defensive cat will react by flattening its ears and dilating its pupils. The first cat will then give the second a full frontal stare prior to a stiffening of the body in preparation for the strike. The ears are up and the tail swishing from side to side. The second cat crouches in deference and averts its head with eyes half closed, its ears flattened and tail on the ground with tip gently flicking up and down.

One of two senarios may follow. The first cat, the aggressor, may advance and the defensive cat may back off, which the first cat may decide is a token of victory and consequently will walk off with a high and mighty expression. The conquered cat will slink away.

Alternatively, cat number two may decide that cat number one is not going to be allowed to get away with a victory, however passive, and so will institute defensive threatening behaviour by bristling its tail and bending it round into an inverted 'U' shape. This cat now becomes the assertive one. It will turn and look back at cat number one with arched back to display aggression, the ears flat and the pupils dilated. But cat number one is not to be deterred by this threatening posture and continues to advance. Cat number two then tries to make its appearance even more threatening by flattening the ears still further and arching the back to a greater

height. The eyes will now be opened as far as possible, accompanied by bared teeth and terrifying hissing. Cat number one is not impressed and continues to approach, by which cat number two is intimidated and falls back with all four paws ready to kick off the assailant, all claws extended. The two cats will contend with each other until the defensive one can see a way to retire with dignity.

Friendly cats that know each other will rub faces and then rub against each other's sides. Sometimes in a multi-cat household a number of the adults will continue to treat each other in similar ways and behave as kittens — greeting, playing, rolling and play-fighting

Cats have a considerable vocabulary when it comes to telling their people what is required to keep them in the manner to which they wish to become accustomed (see Miaow, page 76). Then there are the actions which accompany the sounds or are executed silently — the so-called physical communication. You will find, if you do not know it already, that perseverence and persistence are the watch words with any feline bent on having its own way.

Cats employ various methods of communication in effecting the early morning call. The latter can signify breakfast, time to go out into the garden or simply the time your feline considers you should be out of bed and active.

The first method is simply the most pitiful mewing imaginable, just inside the bedroom door. The next is yet more pitiful mewing, more persistent mewing of a rather more urgent tone with the perpetrator prowling up and down the room or round the bed and back again. This will be maintained until it achieves the desired results.

Quite a number of cats use an object such as a door or window to gain the attention of their person. They do not wish to go through the door or out of the window — these are simply objects to be manipulated to make a noise. Should the door in question be closed, then a rather anti-social method guaranteed to achieve immediate attention is to scratch the carpet just outside the door. This method, whilst foolproof, has its disadvantages — banishment to the kitchen may result or

even loss of other privileges. Some cats will stand on their hind legs and rattle the door handle with a fore paw.

There is a further, somewhat drastic, method reserved for calling to attention the heavy sleeper. The intrepid feline will park itself on the end of the bed and vocalize as loudly as it considers necessary, for as long as necessary. Some masters of method know that there are sleepers for whom the heavier paw is required and have no scruples in executing their plan. First sit on the chest, then pat the cheek gently with one fore paw, claws retracted.

Some cats have been known to pat the eyelids of the sleeper with a feather-light touch. Other cats, it is recorded, actually sit on the head of the recumbent and there are those felines which will sit on the chest and make bread, kneading away to their heart's content, treading up and down until they are quite ecstatic. This is the same motion which kittens employ to stimulate the milk flow when feeding from the queen. In later life, many cats will carry out this procedure on a cushion, bed or lap and are seen to derive considerable pleasure from the exercise.

Feline Friends

Increasingly cats are finding themselves in close proximity to other animals of all kinds, so it is more important than ever for them to be able to live in harmony. If cats are introduced to other animals when they are kittens, better still if the other animals are also young so that they can grow up together, the ensuing relationships will benefit greatly. This is especially so with dogs and cats; they will get to know each other's body language.

The tail is a most important factor. When a dog wags its tail, it is usually a sign of happiness, welcome, excitement etc. On the contrary, when a cat swishes its tail from side to side, it signifies impending strife — by this stage the feline is likely to be very angry indeed.

Kittens and puppies usually get on well together and with reasonable safety if there is not too great a difference in their relative size. A normal adult dog will tolerate a kitten in the same way as it will tolerate a puppy. There is an unwritten code which applies to the young, allowing behaviour from them that would be unacceptable from another adult.

Special care should be taken, though, with any dog which is of the hunting or ratting kind, some of the hounds and terriers. Their instinct, which is inbred, might just lead them to attack a kitten, mistaking it for a rat or the like.

The relationship in reverse, that is an adult cat with a puppy, can be interesting. Some cats will tolerate a puppy but their usual procedure, if they have had enough activity, is to get out of the puppy's way, either by jumping up to a place inaccessible to the puppy, or leaving the room altogether. Some cats, whilst generally well-disposed towards a new puppy in the household, will discipline the youngster if they feel it is taking advantage of its position. This is accomplished by a short, sharp pat on the puppy's hindquarters with a flat paw, no claws extended, making quite a resounding thud.

On occasions the cat might have made such a good job of the procedure that, even when adult, the dog will not pass the cat which is blocking its path·but solicit assistance from a human to intervene.

In the farm kitchen there is a truce, a kind of 'no-man's land' where human laws prevail, not the laws of nature. It is here that the orphaned Muscovy duckling can cuddle up to the farm cat for warmth. On growing up as a pet, this hand-reared creature, with a human mother and sibling dogs and cats, waddles up to greet visitors with the other animals — a duck that thinks it is a cat!

A Toy Poodle of our acquaintance, which lived in a household with a number

of pedigree Persian cats, often had phantom pregnancies when the queens were nursing their kittens. She regularly took over as surrogate mother and actually produced milk. She was a very small Poodle, too small in fact to be bred from, so was able to practise her maternal instincts and achieve satisfaction in association with the kittens. The cream Persian queen, the kitten's mother was quite happy with the arrangements and often shared the feeding with the Poodle.

'The Management of Household Pets', published in 1886, quotes an English magazine of the period, the 'Leisure Hour', which related a fascinating tale of a kitten

and a Kestrel (a small hawk). On the Isle of Wight one brisk afternoon, a lady was taking a walk near the sea when she noticed a small kitten fast asleep on a mossy bank among the rocks. As she approached to stroke the kitten a huge Kestrel swooped as if out of nowhere and alighted between her and the kitten. Fearing the worst she tried to scare off the bird, without success.

In panic, the lady rushed off to some fishermen's cottages nearby to seek assistance, but was unaccountably met with laughter when she recounted her tale. It seems that some time earlier the occupants of the cottages had spied a Kestrel hovering nearby. They began to feed the bird, but noticed that it saved a portion of the food which it flew off with after feeding. Intrigued, they followed the bird and were amazed to see it disappearing into the roof of one of the cottages. Having secured a ladder to investigate they found, nestling in a hole in the roof, a tiny kitten which they rescued and brought back to ground level.

Since that time whenever anyone, especially a stranger, approached the kitten, the Kestrel appeared to exercise his paternal protection rights.

Creatures which we think of as being sworn enemies often seem to be able to live side by side quite happily. Even a cat amongst the pigeons seems as unconcerned as the bird.

There are many tales of bonds of great friendship between cats and horses. The stable cat is often to be found asleep on the back of its favourite horse.

Miaow!

According to documentation in the Louvre in Paris, located by M Champfleury around 1885, the ancient name by which the cat was known was 'mau', 'mai', 'maau' or perhaps 'maou'. Could this be the origin of 'miaow', or has the word simply developed from the sound which the cat makes?

Cats vocalize by air passing over and vibrating the vocal chords in the larynx. They can emit sound on an intake of breath as well as an outgoing one, whereas human beings can only vocalize when breathing out.

Cats possess quite a considerable vocabulary which they can and do use to great effect when dealing with their human associates. They have mews for requests: "Please open the door to let me out", "I want to come in again", "I would like some food", "More food"; those of defence: "Go away", "Don't touch me"; and the polite "Please" and "Thank You".

A cat can shriek with pain or cry out with fear, and a kitten will cry with

that it has its attendant human being totally within its control.

The small, black cat, little more than a kitten, appeared quite suddenly between the balustrades, mewing feebly. How could this little creature be lost at such an age? It was under-weight and wore no collar. It just stood there looking pitiful, yet another city vagrant, cast upon the streets.

To find yourself suddenly among wet leaves on a somewhat chilly autumn day after feeling only warm carpet under paw and other furry bodies next to your own, is rather a shock to the system and not a bit pleasant. It is regrettable that the door was left open permitting escape into an unfamiliar and unwelcoming world.

In the wild wet wood, there was a cat standing in the undergrowth where it had begun to encroach upon the garden of a derelict house: "Keep off, do not come one step nearer. I may be timid, but I can put up a good show."

The vantage point upon the wall was a good one, from which all approaches could be viewed. This was a good position to defend, one from which no contenders would be tolerated.

distress or fear. Cats will hiss or spit in defence or in fear and of course emit that amazing sound which everyone associates with the fireside puss, the inimitable purr.

The cry made by a calling female cat when on heat is a disturbing sound. New owners have been known to contact their veterinarians in panic, thinking that their cat must be in extreme pain.

Then there is the cacophony of sounds commonly known as caterwauling, made by the attendant toms sitting or prowling round a desired female.

Paul Gallico, the esteemed author of many moving stories about animals, especially cats, places considerable emphasis on the 'silent miaow' — guaranteed to produce results in any situation, no matter how unpromising. If you have ever encountered this calculated feline device, when a pathetic cat looks up at its generous and worthy human companion, opens its mouth in characteristic mewing fashion and utters not a sound, you will know that you have been comprehensively compromised. It does not take long for any cat to discover

Catapult

*T*he leaping cat — like a missile released from the sling, it travels through the air with remarkable speed and grace.

The long leap is not one which is often seen by cat watchers in general. Most familiar are those jumps which start from a rear-end-wiggling start on the ground as the cat appears to judge the distance to be leaped, then to charge some sort of imaginary motor for the take-off.

As the cat sails through the air in the long leap, the tail comes upwards until it is at right-angles to the back and in a straight vertical position. As the cat approaches the landing and touch down is achieved, the tail begins to curve over the back. The two fore feet land together first and then the two hind ones. It forms a crouched position to absorb the shock of landing, before striding forward after recovery of the walking, running style.

Cat Burglar

Cats are notorious thieves, even those that are well fed. It is part of their survival mechanism, the instinct to have as much food as possible, whether they can eat it or not or require it or not.

Roger Tabor (see Bibliography, page 144) tells us that Leyhausen's experiment with cats and mice showed that a cat will continue to catch them long after its appetite is sated. Tabor maintains that it is this mechanism which makes the cat rush forward with interest every time the refrigerator door is opened.

Cats will, of course, thieve because they are hungry. Dustbins are raided by feral and semi-feral cats but, given the chance, the well-fed house cat will do the same.

Cats in multi-cat households seem to thieve at every opportunity if any food at all is left unattended, even for a moment, and it seems more difficult to discourage them than a cat in a one-cat household. The latter can be trained or discouraged from going onto tables and work surfaces in the kitchen — it will soon learn which places are unacceptable.

When a well-fed cat develops a voracious appetite and steals food when it has not done so in the past, it is time to start to look for a reason, either physical or psychological.

There are some bold creatures which will steal from under the nose of a poor, well-mannered dog and others for whom nothing is sacred. They will even take the food from the plate in front of you should you relax your vigilance for just a second.

At a dinner party some years ago our host's lilac point Siamese, a most unsociable creature, prowled and gave voice all through the first course. The main course was then served, and our hostess about to take her seat when, with lightning speed, the cat ran along laps from one end of the table to the other, scooping a steak from my plate as she passed and retired under the sideboard, where she could not be reached, with her prize. The action was so fast that the deed was done before anyone realized what was happening.

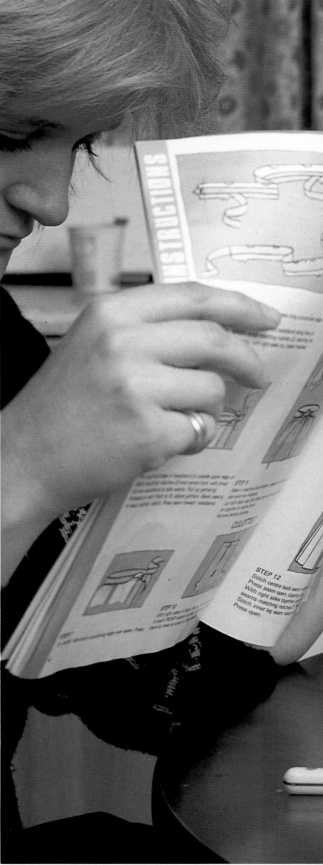

The Cat That Got The Cream

There are many cats which fall on their feet, metaphorically speaking, when they disappear from a former home and go off in search of a new one. Countless cat owners have been known to relate that their cat 'found' them. "It just turned up on the doorstep one day and stayed." Approval was obviously granted. Most of them find themselves wonderful homes where they are petted and doted upon and live on the fat of the land!

Some cats will like milk but many will only drink water. Notwithstanding, most will not turn up their noses if a little cream is offered. For some it is a special treat for high days and holidays. One cat, an all black non-pedigree, who came to us to be photographed in a special way, would

only perform for a lick of cream. He was so possessed with the idea that the mere sight of the carton was sufficient to induce him to come rushing towards us with his tail in the air.

There are those cats which, I am sure you know, have a wonderfully smug, self-satisfied look on their faces, usually when they are trying to confuse the humans after they have been up to mischief of one kind or another. "There's the cat that got the cream," someone will remark, and the Cheshire cat grin will widen still farther.

Some cats will eat with a paw. They will just dip it in, pull it out and lick away to their heart's content. This is especially so when the container is of the narrow-topped variety — a tin of food or perhaps a carton of cream; a container which would make access a little difficult and might just bend up the old whiskers!

Whether the cat has eaten with the paw or not, a good deal of lip-licking and general cleaning up is likely to take place after such a session.

The Cat's Whiskers

"*She thinks she's the cat's whiskers!*" Most cats thinks they are, too.

The length of these very sensitive, specialist 'hairs' (or **vibrissae**) seems to be in direct relationship to the length of hair on the remainder of the cat's body. In other words long-haired cats have longer whiskers than short-haired cats. It may also be that the length of the whiskers is related to the overall size of the cat, since it is believed that cats use their whiskers as a kind of measuring device by which they gauge whether or not they can pass through an opening.

It is important that all the hairs are kept in tip-top condition, whiskers included, so the cat spends a good deal of its waking time in self-grooming. It can wash by licking almost every part of its body, with the exception of the face and ears. These areas are cleansed by the cat licking each fore paw in turn and then rubbing it on the otherwise inaccessible parts.

Playful Cats

_T_he gentle, or in some cases not so
gentle, art of playing is the prime
occupation of kittens. From the moment
they are sufficiently mobile they will chase
their littermate's tail or do battle with the
edge of the blanket. They are at their most
endearing when indulging in their special
antics of rolling, batting, swatting with a
fore paw or pouncing on unsuspecting
'prey'. Two small kittens rolling together
with a good deal of squeaking and
nipping, first one the aggressor then the
other, are laying the foundations in this
'mock' battle for actual combat, when they
reach adulthood.

  Some cats never quite grow out of this
sense of play or perhaps it is used in
adulthood as a substitute for the necessity
of participating in actual hunting
procedures. Many adult cats will play a
little and some play quite a lot. Most cats,
except the few who consider themselves
above such matters, can be induced to play

with a piece of string, a feather, piece of grass or a ball of paper. The instinct to chase and 'kill' any small object which moves in a way similar to that of a small creature, keeping very still and crouched, then indulging in a lightning-flash dart of short duration and so on, will be swiftly followed or pounced upon in the time-honoured fashion.

Siamese and Burmese cats are well known for their abilities in this direction. However, the nimble felines featured here are in fact those exciting and unusual cats, the Turkish Van cats which originate from the shores of Lake Van in Turkey. No matter where an object might fall, these resourceful creatures will seek it out and then return the projectile to the originator, requesting a repeat performance.

This ability to retrieve found in some cats today, mostly the Oriental types and the Turkish, could be a relic of the instinct which the Ancient Egyptians harnessed and exploited when they used the small cats to aid them in the retrieval of small water birds in the reed beds of the Nile.

Cat and Rat

Cats and rats have been sworn enemies since time immemorial and they still are to this day. From the time man first grew grain and began to store it for later use, the rats have followed and the cats have followed the rats.

The rat is a muroid or murine (mouse-like) rodent, especially those of the larger species which infest houses, barns, ships etc. The most prolific is the Common Brown Rat or Norway Rat (**Mus decumanus**), which is a greyish-brown colour on the top of its body and white below, with a comparatively short tail. It is believed to have come originally from western China and where it has been introduced it has supplanted the Black Rat (**Mus rattus**), which is smaller, with larger ears, a more pointed face and longer tail. The Alexandrine Rat, or Roof Rat (**Mus rattus alexandrinus**), is a variety of the Black Rat.

To 'rat' on someone is to be disloyal to someone by giving away secret information about them.

Only once have our paths crossed when, on opening a drain cover to inspect it for damage, there were the two black, beady eyes of a sewer rat. Fortunately, it turned tail and disappeared. On renovating our house a few years ago, when a ceiling was demolished the remains of mouse nests came raining down like confetti, while in another spot the dehydrated, leather-like corpse of a rat was found.

It used to be the custom to build into the structure of a house a cat and a rat, often in the postures of predator and prey. The belief was held that this practice would keep the house free of rats. Juliet Clutton-Brock, in her book 'The British Museum Book of Cats, Ancient and Modern', tells us that this superstition survived quite late into the 18th century, in Britain and all over Europe.

Wherever sea-trade prevailed, cats and rats were present, doing battle and being transported around the known world. In 1665 the most virulent bout of plague reached its peak in London, where one third of the population was wiped out. The Great Plague was carried by the flea which had as its host the brown rat. This

particular rat, transported from the Orient by the trading ships, was a particularly large and vicious strain which, in the war of the rats, defeated and virtually wiped out the black rat. The plague spread over vast areas of the countryside, wiping out entire communities.

It occurs to us to question whether there could be any connection between the witch hunts of the previous one hundred years or so, both the official and unofficial persecution of the cat population, and the serious hold which the plague took in such a short period of time. Did the persecutions make any significant difference to the size of the cat population? In other words, had there been more cats, would there have been significantly fewer rats to spread the plague?

According to Tabor (see page 144) the farmers in the UK today who are reliant on cats for their control of the rat population maintain that, whilst the rats are not entirely eliminated, their numbers

are significantly reduced by employing this traditional method.

Cats and rats are fairly well matched in weight — whilst the cat usually has the advantage, the rat is a formidable adversary.

Having observed the methods used by a cat to stun and then execute a rat, Roger Tabor describes a repetitive tattoo, the cat beating its front paws on the rat many times in succession. The way in which a cat seems to 'play' with a caught mouse, patting it with its front paws, seems to be a modified version of rat-batting.

In these photographs we have the scenario for a tale of mystery and imagination. Is the cat stalking the rat or the rat the cat? Which is the hunter and which the hunted? The strange ancient/modern setting suggests a surreal situation — neither the cat nor the rat is the hunter. There is, instead, a strange conspiracy against the occupants of the house who have left their hearth and home to such strange bedfellows . . .

Top Cats

A high vantage point is a position in which a cat will often be seen. Cats love to be above the world looking down on lesser beings, since this reflects the 'high and mighty' opinion they hold of themselves. It is true that in some cases this self-congratulatory attitude might be justified, for undoubtedly cats are exceedingly clever creatures.

Many of their number have found their way into the annals of history by virtue of their deeds and achievements or by association with the great figures of history, literature and art.

Cardinal Wolsey, Chancellor of England in the reign of Henry VIII (1509-47), was known to share his regal seat with his favourite cat, even during important audiences.

Petrarch, the great Italian poet, thought so much of his cat that he wished it to be venerated for all time so, when the unfortunate creature passed away, he had the body embalmed in the ancient Egyptian style, and placed in a niche in his studio.

Gottfried Mind, the celebrated painter, styled the Raphael of cats, made them his constant study. The poor man was so distraught during the Berne epidemic of hydrophobia that he hid his favourite cat away in the hope of saving its life. This sensitive man never quite recovered from the shock of the destruction of so many cats. He was always found with a cat on his lap or talking to them in his studio when ever anyone called and his large household of cats sat with him while he was painting.

The cat has been immortalized in paint, print and film, from the cartoons of Leonardo da Vinci to the cartoons of Disney.

Chaucer, in the 'Canterbury Tales', immortalizes the cat in the Manciple's Tale . . . 'Lat take a cat and fostre him well with milk . . .' he begins, continuing by encouraging the pampering of the cat with special food and fine silken cushions, all of which the cat rejects in favour of a mousing expedition. This makes it clear that the cat was regarded at this time as a pampered pet.

Théophile Gautier and Voltaire made much of cats and Baudelaire also, to the extent that he was ridiculed in society. Lewis Carroll's 'Cheshire Cat', which was more of a grin and less of a cat, appeared and disappeared right before Alice's astonished eyes in his world-famous children's story of 'Alice in Wonderland'.

T S Eliot's original poetic view of an assortment of cats, a great favourite, has been brought to a new, contemporary audience with resounding success in Andrew Lloyd Webber's musical, 'Cats'.

Many popular cartoon characters have been cats, for example 'Tom' of 'Tom and Jerry', 'Sylvester' and 'Top Cat'. Cats have also taken the starring role in many block-busting animated feature films, such as 'Aristocats' and more recently, 'Oliver and Company'. The comic strip character, Korkey the Cat, has entertained generations. The Walt Disney tear-jerker, 'Tomasina' (not animated), based on a story by Paul Gallico about a little girl and a red tabby cat, was a family favourite.

Television commercials for cat food, carpets and toilet tissue continue to bring the most beautiful and able cats into our homes and contemporary life.

A top cat with a sense of humour and the last word in vantage points. It seems

that we can say with safety that we have seen it all! Hats off to this one! How high is it possible to climb and still retain one's dignity? The ceiling must be the limit.

To exit stage 'up and over' is the way most cats would go, given the excuse to climb, through the smallest opening.

The fan-light route is a favourite exit for those of athletic inclination and not a bad place for a rest for those with a predeliction for such apparently uncomfortable perches.

It is here amongst the tiles, the mansards and the chimney stacks that a land exists known only to the feline race; and sadly to the tiny child chimney sweeps of the 19th century, to Fagin's boys in Charles Dickens' 'Oliver Twist' and to those thieves and burglars of an athletic bent. Caterwauling on the cat walks, frisking on the fire escapes, or a tête-à-tete amongst the television aerials all goes to prove that if you have the nerve to do it you can make it to the top!

Cats on Watch

Watching and waiting. Waiting and watching. Activities at which cats everywhere excel.

"We watch on the ground, we watch from the roof tops. Whatever there is to see, we will see it. We see all, miss nothing in the blink of an eye on a lazy summer afternoon when you think us snoozing. 'That lazy cat', we hear you pronounce to a guest, 'sitting around all day'. Little do you know what a mountain of information we have accumulated through our eyes, our noses, our ears and our whiskers."

They have watched the dawn of history, seen the leopards leap and, been party to the seven wonders of the world. They have seen the Pharohs come and go, and sat on deck and watched the seven seas roll by with explorers on voyages of discovery, conquerors and empire-builders as well as traders.

They have peered from darkened corners while witch-hunters passed by and waited for renaissance day to dawn; watched history in the making from beside the ruler's throne and passed the time away in the company of great men.

With patience and fortitude, the remarkable cat has sat out the measured passage of the sands of time through centuries of adoration, persecution, adulation and admiration; persevered throughout the atrocities of fanatacism and suffered all kinds of savage treatment and deprivation from the hand which stroked it.

Now it waits for the day to dawn when all of its number, high or lowly, fat or thin will be able to eat their fill, sit in comfort, without fear or favour and just watch and wait . . .

Cool Cats

With apologies to Tennessee Williams, our 'Cat on a Hot Tin Roof' is one of quite a different colour. A favourite feline lounging location would be just such a stretch of corrugated iron found on many a humble shack. Even a few rays of watery sunshine can make all the difference to the comfort of a care-worn street cat when enhanced by the metal surface of the roof.

Lazy, hazy, crazy days of summer — early summer, perhaps not quite so hazy, with the daisies and celandine peeping through the grass. This is a perfectly peaceful place to lounge and then snooze, eyes half closed for maximum effect, with body stretched out to allow some of the heat to escape.

The beam high up in the roof of the barn is an ideal spot for a morning away from the mêlée of life outside. The fur is puffed up to retain as much of the warm air rising from below as possible.

Cats seem to like to be where the fresh air can reach them even though they may not be totally out in the open, although many a cat will sit on an exposed rail, fence or wall in the most inclement weather conditions.

Boss Cats

In an enclosed area where a number of cats live as a group it has been found that a strict order of dominance, ie a feline hierarchy, is established. This is evident from the postures which the cats adopt in relation to their height above ground level. Therefore, the cat occupying the highest point is the boss cat, the highest in the pecking order.

In a group where there are un-neutered and neutered individuals, the 'boss' cat will almost certainly be an entire male.

In a cat sanctuary, with an enclosed and occasionally changing population of mostly unrelated cats, very little aggression takes place, except for minor scraps instigated by cats which gain themselves the title of 'trouble-maker' as a result. In a situation where food is always available to all in plentiful supply, aggression over competition for food is eliminated.

A social hierarchy still exists in this kind of colony with one, or sometimes two dominant cats — usually males (all cats are neuters within the sanctuary).

Nocturnal Cats

Would you not like to be a fly on the wall and observe your cat when it ventures out on nocturnal jaunts? Where does it go and what does it do when it gets there?

Night enfolds like a blanket and covers a multitude of sins. When most of the population has gone to bed or is preoccupied with television or other pursuits, there are wayward souls on the move. Early in the night, a favoured time of day for hunting, the urban feral cats are beginning to bestir themselves for their nightly excursions.

Many of the feral colonies include cats which are so shy of people that the only time you will see any of them is at night. Auxiliary feeders take supplies to the area where they know the cats are located and retire to observe from the sidelines. Cats will appear from their hiding places to eat the food. Once a feeding time has been established, the cats will be waiting when that time draws near.

It is usually at night that these worthy souls, the feeders, do such sterling work for these unfortunate felines. They leave their suppers and beds regularly to feed the hungry multitudes in towns and cities the world over.

In order to contain the otherwise exploding cat population, a neutering campaign has been firmly established in London and other British cities, across Europe: Amsterdam, Monaco, Florence, Venice and in the South of France. The trapped cats are neutered, given a health check and kept until fully recovered and then returned to the location from which they were taken. It is the usual practice to tip the edge of one ear so that the cats that have already been neutered can be identified from a distance, to avoid them being trapped a second time.

Feral cat colonies in rural communities may not be so fortunate in having human assistance with their survival programme. In this case, they have to rely on live prey for their existence.

Copy Cat

One activity in which cats do not seem to engage is copying, anyone or anything else.

So, how did this well-known phrase originate? It does seem to be a long-standing children's chant. "Copy cat, copy cat" can still be heard resounding in children's playgrounds and school-rooms. Copying homework, schoolwork, a game, a way of dressing — it denotes an inability to be original or to think for oneself.

Two uncorroborated theories have been put forward on the derivation of 'copy cat'. The first denies any connection with cats. It suggests that the derivation is from an early copying machine, produced by a company called Katz. 'Katz copies' could be quickly reversed to become 'copy cats'.

The second theory is that the phrase is a derivative of 'Catechism', which was taught in schools. A credited shortening of the word is 'Cat'. In order that the Catechism could be more easily learnt, or as a punishment for not having learnt it satisfactorily, pupils were instructed to 'copy' the text in their notebooks, or parts of it — copy the Cat . . . copy cat.

Having failed to isolate any behaviour of the copying kind in the cat, such as to 'ape' or imitate, the only conclusion I can reach is that the cat is above all a creature of habit. Once a cat has formed a sequence of behaviour and a way of carrying out its daily routine, it tends to follow in its own footsteps, copy its own actions from day to day. That is the only sense in which the cat could be called a copy cat.

Cat Beauty

In the unlikely event of a testimonial being requested to the beauty and vitality of the ever captivating cat, one would simply refer to the work of the great company of painters, sculptors, writers and poets who have exercised their art over the centuries, depicting in glowing terms all the attributes of this most compelling, elusive of creatures.

It does not necessarily take the anatomical accuracy and expression of movement of Leonardo da Vinci, the intimate drawings of Gottfried Mind or the modern, colourful naivety of Martin Leman to portray the many subtle facets of feline grace — or indeed the penmanship of Théophile Gautier, Edgar Allan Poe or the searching sensitivity of Paul Gallico to bring the character of the cat to the fore. But they and all the other felinophiles who have expressed themselves on the subject have their contribution to make to the expanding fund of information.

Perhaps the key lies in the unblinking stare of the cat's eye, the lush pile of the velvet fur, the suppleness of movement. Or in that indefinable spark of presence, which can make even the ugly beautiful, which gives rise to the compulsion to try to hold captive the beauty of the captivating cat.

Cats' Eyes

All kittens have blue eyes which change to their adult colour when they are about three months old. Cats' eyes vary in colour from deep amber through all shades of orange and yellow, from pale green to deep emerald green; sea green/blue to pale, medium and deep blue. Some cats have eyes of more than one colour — greenish orange flecked with deeper orange and yellowish green. Some have a spangled effect and most will have variations of

tones of the colour depending from which angle and in which lighting they are viewed. Some white cats have odd coloured eyes — one orange or yellow and one blue.

The cat's eye has an upper and lower lid, well furred with longer hair on the edges (lashes) which serve to protect the eye. The cat also has a 'third eyelid', the nictitating membrane which comes across the eye from the centre corner outwards covering about two-thirds of the visible part of the eye when fully extended. Under normal circumstances it is not visible, but on occasions comes into view either partially or to its full extent. This happens when a cat is ill and is, in fact, one of the first signs of ill-health in a cat. It also seems to show itself a little when the cat is stressed, but should return to normal when the source of the anxiety is identified and dealt with.

The cat cannot focus very well on objects which are close to it, but has a more well-defined focus at a distance. Apparently it sees best at a distance of around 2 to 6 metres (7 to 20 feet).

There are light sensitive receptors at the back of the eye which respond to various colours of the spectrum. The cat possesses receptors sensitive to blue and yellow, but not those sensitive to red.

It is commonly said that cats can see in the dark. This is not exactly true, since there must be a small amount of light present. A cat cannot see in total darkness, but it is certainly able to see in very low-light conditions, those which a human eye would detect as pitch darkness.

The pupil, the black area in the centre of the eye, opens and closes according to the amount of light present. In poor lighting conditions, it will open up and become almost round in appearance, as large as 12 millimetres (½ inch), and in very bright light it will close to a slit, or even close altogether, leaving only a pinhole at the top and bottom.

It operates in a similar way to the lens of a camera, the open position corresponding to a large aperture (or 'F' number). The large aperture lets in more light to fall on the film at the back of the camera, just as the light passing through the pupil carries the image onto the retina at the back of the eye. The photographic image is stored on the film until processed; the image on the retina is transmitted through the optic nerve to the 'viewing' part of the brain, where it is

'seen'. Also, the image projected on to the retina of the cat's eye is five times brighter than that of the human eye.

Cats' eyes shine in the dark, like pinpoints of light glowing out of the darkness. Cats with orange eyes and those with green eyes glow green or turquoise; those with blue eyes glow red when a light source, such as a flash light or the headlamps of a car, is shone on them.

The mirror-like lining of the retina at the back of the eye, **tapetum lucidum**, reflects light from outside the eye which has not been absorbed on the first passage through the eye. The retina receives a second stimulation from this 'residue' light, thus increasing the eye's sensitivity in dim light.

This reflection of light on the retina is also responsible for cats' eyes glowing red or green when a photograph of the cat is taken with a single flash light.

This reflectability was spotted by the man who invented the **Cats' Eyes**, the small reflective markers used on our roads making them visible at night in the beam of the headlamps of a car.

Black and White Cats

A juxtaposition of black and white is the most extreme contrast you will ever see — that which absorbs the most light set beside that which reflects the most light.

Black is the symbol of darkness, fear, night, evil, sleep, enveloping oblivion and good fortune, should a cat of that colour cross your path. White is associated with light, piety and purity.

The infinite variety of black and white or 'Magpie' cats is remarkable, from those with only a tiny white locket on the chest, through the variations of white nose, bib and feet, to the half and half bi-colour markings, sought after by the pedigree cat breeders.

Black and white cats, whether pedigree (of which there are very few) or non-pedigree in their infinite variety of size, appearance and markings, are perhaps the most dramatic and beautiful of all cats. As 'designer' cats, they could not have been better portrayed had they come straight off the drawing board itself.

deep orange-copper eye colour which is exclusive to the breed. The Blue Long-hair (Persian) is the only other blue cat with orange-copper eyes.

The Korat, from Thailand, known there for hundreds of years as 'Si-Sawat', is another short-haired blue. The Russian Blue is a most distinctive creature. Originally called the Archangel Cat, it is slimmer than the British or the Korat, more elongated and elegant although not quite so svelt as the Siamese, which also boasts a blue self version in the shape of the Foreign (Oriental) Blue. A quality Russian, say for showing purposes, has a distinctive heart-shaped face and emerald green eyes, while the Foreign Blue is permitted to have green or amber eyes.

The are also blue Burmese as well as all the breeds which have self colours and bi-colours — the Manx, Maine Coon, etc. There are blue tabbies, blue smokes, pointed, as in Siamese and Colourpoints (Himalayan) and dilute tortoiseshells.

Even the humble non-pedigree will be present in this illustrious group, but will probably have a portion of white somewhere on the body, even if it is only a spot on the chest or perhaps a portion of white on the chin. It is most likely to have green eyes.

Next time you see a humble grey cat disappearing into the shadows, be sure to acknowledge it as a 'Super Blue'.

Super Blues

The super blues are cats to look up to; cats of character and superiority. Whether Foreign, British or non-pedigree, they all have the same genetic colouring. Because the blue coat colouring is a natural mutation, a dilute form of black, it can occur in any breed.

Self-coloured blue cats — the non-initiated would call them grey — have occurred naturally all over the world. The coat colour is actually a slate blue-grey varying in tone from a pale delicate shade to quite a dark tone, including all the shades and tones in-between.

The British Blue has a wonderfully thick, bushy coat, a big, full face and solid bone structure. Its distinguishing feature, for instant recognition, is the wonderful

Cat Lives

This is the lifestyle of the cat in clover, the one that always gets the cream, perfectly endowed in every direction, warm and comfortable with plenty to eat and even some to spare. This is the cat that is well cared for, its health a subject for concern; well groomed and presented on every occasion, nails clipped and whiskers preened. This is the cat that has its own place, furnished to the highest standards; the designer cushion, with the four-poster bed as an 'extra'.

This is the cat that travels by taxi or sometimes takes trips in a plane; has its own toothbrush, health insurance and accident cover. This is the cat about which cults are cultivated, depicted in china and glass, plaster and stone, engraved, painted, embroidered, drawn and its virtues extolled in just about every language under the sun. This

perfect creature has every advantage in life, is feted, adored and even worshipped — the proverbial fat cat from which a thin one is trying to escape.

This is the cat that skulks in corners and takes flight at human approach. Its lack-lustre coat and dull eye betray illness, hunger or age.

This is the cat with a place of its own — a corner of a derelict building or a pile of sacking in a barn. This is the cat that hunts for its food to survive, whose palace is an abandoned place or the great outdoors.

This is the cat that travels on foot, sliding in and out of the shadows to avoid detection, crossing and recrossing its tried and tested paths of habit and safety. Its days are filled with coming and going; with watching, waiting and sitting, crouched in the dead leaves or

combinations and varieties of these flavours; dried food products and semi-moist varieties. For the sick cat there are ranges of specialist prescription foods, prepared to meet the specific needs of animals with medical problems, for example heart disease, kidney disease, etc. There are also diets for cats convalescing after an illness. There are various dietary supplements for use during periods of growth — for kittens and adolescents — when extra nutrients, vitamins, etc are required; for pregnant and nursing queens and for the cat in old age. Also available are supplements to improve the cat's general well-being as well as the condition and appearance of the coat.

As far as external appearance is concerned there are many ranges of products, from shampoos of several kinds — some purely cosmetic, or herbal, medicated, etc — to powders and sprays to use against parasites in the fur. Some of these products will be available across the counter in pet stores and specialist pet departments in major stores, by mail order and a number exclusively available through a veterinarian.

gazing empty-eyed from a decaying, glassless window.

This is the almost forgotten cat, the one that has nearly slipped into the grey areas of non-profit, the bureaucratic oblivion of nuisance value, the unwelcome statistic. Fortunately there are a few people in many countries whose watchword is concern, who care and will give freely of that most precious of intangibles in this modern age — their time.

With their help and a lot more, it may be possible to envisage the day when outside every thin cat there will be a fat one waiting to get in.

_____ *Fat Cats* _____

The cat cannot have been better cared for than it is today, with more facilities and products available on the market than ever before.

As far as feeding is concerned, there are canned foods of meat, fish and

To care for the cat's health, veterinarians are required to complete several years of training at college, together with experience gained in practice. Preventative veterinary medicine is well to the fore today with the availability of vaccines for major feline killer diseases. Where accident and disease do occur, veterinarians are eminently disposed to offer treatment in the form of medication or surgery, should it be necessary, and information on an animal's particular problems. The best way to avail yourself of this professional service is to register your pet as soon as you acquire it with a veterinarian in your locality.

For the comfort and edification of the discerning feline, the market is well supplied with a variety of accommodation for slumber and snoozing alike. If one wishes to be traditional, there are wicker baskets of various sizes. For the more hygienically-minded, rigid plastic cat beds are available, which can be easily disinfected, an assortment of filled fabric beds in all colours and designs including fur fabric, or an easily-maintainable bean bag, in appropriate sizes. Recent innovations include some exotically-designed relaxing containers, to be fixed onto a radiator or to fit just beneath one; some to hang, some to swing in hammock fashion for extra comfort and fun. Some are available with their own travelling cover, so puss can be transported, bed and all. Lastly, there are carrying cases made in plastic which bisect into top and bottom, the base becoming a bed.

Transportation is a major factor in a cat's life, even if it is only a veterinary visit for a booster vaccination; the safest method is in a closed container. Again, the traditional wicker basket is available, some enclosed and some with a grill at one end to afford a view for the cat and enable the owner to see inside to check on puss's condition. Some cats become quite stressed on journeys, but most take it in their stride, especially if they are introduced to travel at an early age. There are plastic-covered wire baskets, rectangular or arched, rigid plastic, clear plastic, those which open into beds and even some made of cardboard, for limited use or emergency.

Just in case, within this busy life of eating, sleeping, travelling and being beautified, your cat has a few moments to

call its own, the thoughtful manufacturers have provided toys to attract and console, exercise and amuse. Balls on elastic, fabric mice, things to bat, to pounce upon, to throw and to leap for. Climbing apparatus of several kinds, shelves to sit upon to look down on the lowly world below. There are boxes with holes to climb in and out and a number of different designs of scratching post on which to strop the claws, in place of the wallpaper, door frame or sofa.

For those most fortunate of felines whose living space is nothing short of a stately home, one may visit the library, to improve one's education, absorb all that knowledge from the comfort of a cushion-bound sofa, or appreciate a prelude or two on the grand piano, admire the fine china

and silver or regard the family portrait with aplomb.

Alternatively, on a fine afternoon, a stroll across the velvet sward towards the perimeter of the grounds might be a change, to follow one's nose to where the wild things live, to be only a whisker away from the woods and the fields, the farm and the factory, the town and the back yards where the other half lives . . .

Thin Cats

Many people think, mistakenly, that the term 'feral' applies to the wild cat, the indiginous wild cat of any country or continent. This is, in fact, not so. The feral is the cat which has been domesticated at some time, even if this was several or many generations before, and has turned to the wild for its habitat. This 'wild' may be countryside in the rural sense, suburban open spaces, hospital grounds or those of some other institution, urban wasteland, inner-city yard or garden square.

'The Management of Household Pets', 1862, tells us that the Turks were great admirers of cats and that when Baumgarten visited Damascus he found a hospital for cats. The legend goes that the Prophet, Mohammed, once lived in a house on the site and he had such a high regard for cats that, rather than disturb one which had fallen asleep on the sleeve of his robe, he cut the sleeve off. His followers set up a sanctuary for sick cats, which was funded by public alms.

In an apothecary's window a couple of centuries earlier, a notice could be seen — 'Axungia cati sylvestris: extract of wild cat, a certain cure for lameness, epilepsy etc.' Many parts of the cat were used for medicines and potions.

The true wild cat of Europe is the Forest Wild Cat, **Felis sylvestris sylvestris** and related sub-species (**grampia, caucasia** etc). Guggisberg tells us that it is approximately one third larger than the common, domestic cat, sturdier with longer legs, a broader head and a tail that is thicker with a blunt end. The coat is a dense fur with a ground colour of yellowish grey, darker and more greyish on the back and more yellowish to cream on the underside with a white throat. There are four or five longitudinal stripes from the forehead to the nape of the neck merging into one dark, dorsal line to the root of the tail. From the dorsal line several transverse lines run down the sides to the belly. The tail has several encircling lines, two or three real circles and a dark tip. The legs have several transverse stripes and a spot on the base of the fifth toe of the hind feet. The nose is flesh coloured, there are 30 teeth and eight teats. Its young are more distinctly marked than the adult and can at three to nine months be easily mistaken for a domestic tabby. Even in adults the difference is not so clear cut as might be expected. Early records of wild cats in the Bernese and Pennine Alps of Switzerland are now known to be conclusively of feral domestic cats.

Earlier this century Kenneth Richmond, in 'Wild Animals of Britain', published in 1946, described his view of the Scottish Wild Cat, **Felis sylvestris grampia**, which he admits to having seen only once through field glasses on the mountain Ben MacDhui, in Invernesshire. He described it as heavier than the fireside tabby with a more tigerish head and thicker tail. Originally a forest dweller he wrote that it is now driven to remote parts and the wilder mountains and moorlands of the northern-most parts of Scotland. Its prey are the blue mountain hare, the white winged ptarmigan and hillside voles but

will come down to the wooded areas for squirrels and rabbits. Writing in 1946, Richmond suggested that the wild cat has two litters per year. Guggisberg puts it at one, except where the climate allows two.

Many of the large cities across the world and also many rural areas have a feral cat population. Only in areas where the cats impinge on man's living space do we find that a problem has been recognized.

Many of these cats lead a twilight existence, particularly in the inner-city areas, especially those who are banished to the under-world of a large institution's heating system.

In London, Amsterdam, Monaco and Venice, to name only a few of the cities in question, the various organizations which have been set up by concerned individuals are engaged on a feeding, trapping and neutering campaign, treating for illness and returning cats to the locations from which they were taken.

Thin Cats

The cats of Venice are a special case in that their feral cat problem was man-made by the importation of cats from Syria to solve, so it was thought, the rat problem. The organization DINGO has and is still doing as much as it can to help alleviate the problems there. An island in the lagoon, Lazaretto Vecchio, acquired by the animal painter, Gina Fiera, homes both stray cats and dogs. There are several other organizations working in Venice and on the mainland, including a branch of the anti-vivisection league, working for the protection and alleviation of the suffering of the cats of Venice.

When one thinks of the Principality of Monaco, an image immediately springs to mind of waving palm trees along the harbour, the bright lights of the casinos and the fairy-tale palace set high up on the rock of the old town. In the exotic gardens one encounters cryptic notices relating the location of 'cat feeding places'.

These turn out to be part of a happy scheme which seems to have solved the problems of not only the feral cat population but also the wonderful band of feeding ladies and the immense number of tourists who visit the Principality.

As the moving force behind the Monegasque equivalent of the RSPCA, Her Serene Highness Princess Antoinette of Monaco, an ardent cat and dog lover, has founded a sanctuary for both cats and dogs at her villa half-way up the steep Alpes Maritimes overlooking the Mediterranean along the coast of France. There, several hundred animals lead happy, contented lives cared for by two veterinary nurses from Scotland. Some of the cats there are Monegasque and some are cats of the locality. "They hear about us somehow, and just turn up at the gate," maintains the Princess.

The Monegasque rescue and neutering campaign has been and is continuing to be successful. The auxiliary feeding ladies, who used to take so much pleasure in being able to help the cats, still do so but in the beautifully organized way which has been devised in special places, discreetly, at set times of day and in dark-coloured containers.

Next time a cat is spied sitting on a wall or fence or crossing a piece of wasteland, running down an alley or scavenging from a market anywhere in the world, it might be worth sparing a thought to consider if it has a home to go to.

Water Cats

Amsterdam, the Venice of the north, with its web of beautiful canals set out by order of the Burgomaster in 1612 to expand the town at the beginning of the so-called Golden Age. There are wide canals and narrower ones supporting the tall, slender houses so typical of the city, warehouses, churches and more than 1,000 bridges all flanked by many rows of elm trees. Moored along the banks of the canals are countless barges populated by families with their children and of course their dogs and cats.

Over the years, Amsterdam has been a haven for people from all over Europe and beyond, seeking asylum from religious and other persecution, many of whom expanded its wealth and population. At one time it was the third city of Europe, after London and Paris.

So it is following an historical tradition for sanctuary to be offered to those in need in Amsterdam. Below the formidable facades of the tall, slender houses which overlook the gently lapping waters of Singel Canal lie the barges and houseboats, moored inches apart, bow to stern — the lower-level inhabitants of this water street. One of these, lying long and low in the water, boasts a very strange cargo indeed, a population of feline souls, living here in the kind of luxury of which the ocean-going stowaways of days of yore could only dream.

Safe and sound within this sanctuary of some 20 years' duration live these waifs and strays from the back streets and gardens which are taken onboard to be cared for with much expertise and tender loving care.

This is none other than the world-famous Cat Boat of Amsterdam, De Poezenboot. Cat lovers from all corners of the globe visit the houseboat every year, which operates entirely on donations from the public. It is moored on the Singel, opposite number 40, with a further houseboat moored nearby.

The boat and the programme of neutering the cats and returning those ferals to their original environment is the brain-child of Henriette van Weelde who inadvertently, some 45 years ago, took on a big responsibility when she rescued her first cat. Appalled and upset by the tragic way people maltreated and abandoned their cats, she resolved to do something to help. Now, all these years later, there are two houseboats on the canal, an extensive neutering campaign throughout Amsterdam and a farm on the outskirts near Hoorn, which the Poezenboot Foundation owns, where another 120 cats are cared for.

Henriette, now in her 70's, keeps the cats for five to ten years since she does not believe in passing them on. Only if a prospective owner can convince her of their good intent will she permit them to take one of her cats. In order to help fund the neutering, which is expensive, as well as the upkeep of the cats, there is an 'adopt a cat' programme, offering a newsletter and a Christmas card with a photo of 'your' cat sent to each sponsor.

The Poezenboot has an extensive interior area — light, bright and hygienic,

with a tiled floor, walls and a black stove, the latter being a great favourite with the cats. It is surrounded by their rigid plastic beds and circular chairs, promoting a cosy, relaxed, lounge-like atmosphere where the cats are very much at home. Close by there is a most ingenious device for utilizing space in a relatively limited area: a series of shelves stacked one upon the other open at all four sides thus allowing the cats to climb from one level to another to sit or to feed. Outside on the terrace, only the safety netting comes between the cats and the view over the waters of the canal where they can sit or promenade, as the mood takes them.

The population appears to be mostly short-haired, with some tabbies, the occasional red tabby and white but with black and white predominating.

At feeding time every one takes to their own dish of tinned delight with relish, well spaced out, then a short snooze or siesta either inside or out, as the mood or the weather dictates, and then perhaps it will be time for a few more visitors to come to wonder and admire this very special floating population.

Traditionally, water is anathema to cats. Mention it in their presence and you will

get very short shrift indeed. A dainty feline will not put its nose outside the door if there is even the merest hint of rainfall and will pick its way around the smallest puddle, where the canine counterpart will unconcernedly splash through the deepest part. However, paradoxically, most of the cats I know will happily sit out in the rain for hours with apparent unconcern when the mood takes them. Certainly, even the most thorough soaking our long-haired non-pedigree has ever had has not penetrated further than the surface hair. The pads on the underside of cats' feet, however, are exceedingly sensitive, so perhaps the avoidance of puddles is understandable in view of this fact.

Full immersion is another matter altogether. Most cats will swim if they have to and a few will do it from choice. A long-haired tabby I knew had to be locked out of the bathroom to exclude her from sharing ablutions with anyone who happened to be in occupancy.

Those cats which are actually reputed to enjoy swimming are the exotic Turkish Van cats. They originated on the shores of Lake Van in Turkey and are related to the Angora cats. These cats were supposed to indulge in aquatics in the sparkling shallows on the shores of Lake Van.

The 'Turks', as they are affectionately known, are the most endearing but active cats. Pure white semi long-haired cats with silky, easily-maintained fur, boasting spectacular auburn bushy tails and distinctive auburn head markings, they swim from choice. One of the original breeders of these exciting cats in the UK said that her cats were happier if the sun was shining and sparkling on the surface of the water.

Whether the dip is in a special pond, the bath or a grand, full-size swimming pool, when a cat is swimming it folds its ears backwards, flat against the head to stop the water from entering. When the cat emerges from the water, stand well back, for an elaborate shaking to dispel the water from the coat will take place, as in the case of any dog.

While the bubbles might be fun to play with, a bathful of clear fresh water is to be preferred, although the ideal is in the great outdoors on a warm, sunny day — not dissimilar to our human preferences.

We all know the call of the sea — the wonderful, invigorating scent of ozone, the rolling waves crashing onto the beach and the unmistakable, rhythmic sound of the tide draining through the shingle as it recedes.

Around coastlines there are many cats living close to the beach. In some fishing areas, the fishermen's cottages back straight onto the shore, sometimes with a drop down to the sea from the wall of the back yard. It was (and still is in some

parts) where the fish were gutted and the remains tossed over the wall back into the sea for the gulls to swoop and cry as they scavenged the trimmings from the surface of the sea.

Cats have a long history of seafaring connections. It was a time-honoured tradition to take a cat on board ship and a sign of good fortune — not to mention the advantage of having a captive rodent controller.

It was said, in nautical circles, that if the ship's cat became highly active and started to rush about madly, it signified an impending storm.

Of the small wild cats, the Fishing Cat (**Prionailurus viverrinus**) is directly concerned with water. Found in India and the Far East, this cat frequents mangrove swamps, lake fringes, creeks, ocean inlets and small streams. It is larger than most of the small wild cats, being 38

centimetres (15 inches) to the shoulder and very powerful and fierce.

Guggisberg ('Wild Cats of the World', 1975) tells us that W G Adams observed one of these cats in Ceylon, sitting on a sand bank scooping fish out of the water with its fore paw, which has definite webbing between the toes and claws which are slightly too long to be completely sheathed. It acted in a similar way to a domestic cat trying to scoop a fish out of the goldfish tank, or pond. He maintained that the cat went into quite deep water. It is now known that the fishing cat will wade into the water and there have been reports of it actually diving for prey. It also takes snails, snakes, frogs and small mammals and was once reported to have carried off a four month-old baby which, fortunately, was rescued alive.

Domestic pet cats have quite a reputation for fishing and will spend many hours crouched by the side of the fish pond in the garden in the hope that a fish will come within reach of the ever-ready paw poised above. To discourage this habit, many garden ponds are covered with a layer of netting stretched across the surface of the water.

Many seaside cats will hang around the fishing boats in the hope that some tit-bit will come their way, or perhaps a short sea trip to blow away the cobwebs.

Farm Cats

The cat, although so much a creature of habit, is nevertheless an animal that is able to adapt its ways to all manner of environments, literally from the drawing room to the farmyard.

It is equally at home perched upon a hay bale high up in a barn, awaiting its chance to catch a small creature unawares, to reclining upon a silken cushion before a roaring fire.

To pick its way across a half frozen farmyard, negotiating the melting ice between the peaks of frozen mud thrown up by the livestock's hooves, can be part of the everyday routine in the 'down-to-earth' life of a farm cat.

It might spend hours sitting in the barn just waiting for that mouse or rat to show itself, if it dares. The mere presence of a cat on the premises is often sufficient to deter vermin, although the chances are that there will be quite a line-up laid out for inspection by breakfast time.

Perhaps a visit to the burrows on the edge of the wood is the next port of call to reconnoitre the land for a twilight raid.

Down on the farm, and in rural areas in general, the cat will have the opportunity to hunt a wider variety of creatures.

The farmer's attitude to animals tends to differ considerably from that of the pet owner. Except in unusual situations, farm cats are workers, kept to control the all-important problem of the rodent population, even today a very real one.

Working Cats

The concept of the cat as a working animal, that is one which earns its keep, is not a new one. The title of vermin exterminator extraordinaire in exchange for a saucer of cream and a place by the fire has a lengthy history. Only during the periods of time when the cat has been extolled as a god, taken into the home as a pet and for approximately the past 100 years or so, has it not been a totally working animal.

But, surprisingly, there are many organizations and places of work where there is a cat 'on the staff'. Barracks with stables and grain to protect, schools and colleges, offices, factories and warehouses, as well as theatres and museums — all these sites offer work for the willing feline. Even the official home of the British Prime Minister, 10 Downing Street, has employed several cats over the years, one at a time. A sum of money was allocated for their upkeep and they were looked after by the housekeeper.

There have always been resident cats at railway stations. One which immediately comes to mind, simply because it was famous and used to receive mail from all over the world, was the exceedingly fat cat that resided for many years in the ladies' cloakroom at Paddington Station, London. There was also a black and white cat called Sam who had his house, a cardboard box with his name over the entrance, at the end of a platform near the buffers at Kings Cross Station, also in London.

Church Cats

To be 'as poor as a church mouse' was to be poor indeed. The pickings to be found in a Christian place of worship, except perhaps at Harvest Thanksgiving, were surely minimal. So, the church cat's existence in days of yore, when cats were expected to fend for themselves, must have been a thin one.

There was a time when it would have been sacrilegious to permit a cat access to a sanctified place. Fortunately, people today see the cat in a totally different light. There are many churches, even cathedrals, which have a cat in residence; some enjoy the company of several cats, including Westminster Abbey in London.

Many churches also hold a special service when pets of all kinds, including cats of course, can be brought to be blessed. At Florence in Italy, in the church of St Lorenzo, the cloister has, over the years, become a place of sanctuary for lost or unwanted cats.

The Tail-end

There are tales and there are tails and there are tales about tails and so **ad infinitum** . . .

The tail is a continuation of the spine, containing 21 to 24 coccygeal vertebrae, depending on its length. Oriental types have long, tapering tails, accentuated by close-lying, smooth hair. Persian tails are shorter, with full, flowing hair, while British Shorthairs have thicker tails covered with bushy fur. All other pedigree types and all non-pedigrees come somewhere between these extremes, depending on body conformation and coat type. The Japanese Bobtail is a breed with a tail about half the length of other cats,

whilst the Manx is tail-less. Those cats with small protuberances where the tail would commence are known as Rumpies and Stumpies.

A feature of the balance and beauty of the cat, the tail is a notable indication of mood and intent. From the first time a kitten is induced to attack by pouncing on its mother's provocatively twitching tail to that supreme moment when your cat approaches, tail erect with the tip slightly curved over in that characteristic feline greeting, it is clear that this elegant appendage is much more than simply 'that which comes behind'!

So that, in the end, we hope that we will be able to say, not without conviction, that hereby hangs the tale of these endearing, captivating cats.

Acknowledgments

The author and photographer would like to thank the following: Mr Buckler; Mr and Mrs Childerhouse; John and Phyllis Choppen; Mary Creggan; Anna Gainsford; Bill and Mary Geering; Catherine Hardie; Anna Hill; Emma Hoare; Carol Jones; Miranda von Kirchberg; Brenda Parkes; Sue Payne; Denise Reed; Anita Rowsell; Judy Shepherd; Vi Warriner; Annette West; Mike Wood. Special thanks for their help go to: Abyssinian Cat Club; Ashfold Preparatory School, Dorton House; Nikki Barrass; Lady Beaverbrook and household; Bellmead — David and Angela Cavill; Bernadette Benson; Bermans and Nathans, London — theatrical hire; Cat Action Trust — Elke de Vries; Cat Fax; Janet Colchester; De Poezenboot — Judith, her associate and Henriette van Weelde; Julian and Joan Delf; The Dogs' Home, Battersea; Margaret and Peter Frayne; Dolores Gatti; Diana Harper; Cheryl and Brett Hassell; Pat Humphries; Kirsty; Lois Miles; Pam Pickering; Bernard and Alison Plumb and all the people and their cats too numerous to mention; Her Serene Highness Princess Antoinette of Monaco; Morag Robertson; St Mary the Virgin, Ludgershall, Bucks; Molga Salvalaggio; Denise and Ernest Speller; Kay Spencer-Barnard; Stoke Mandeville Hospital. Extra special thanks go to: Alison Graham, Public Relations, for her support; Kodak Ltd and Fuji Photo Film Co Ltd for their excellent film; Hasselblad, Sweden and Nikon, UK for cameras; Sky Photographic and Ceta Colour Laboratories for processing the film; Joe Gahan for safe transportation to and from locations and for all his additional assistance; Jo Finnis and Nigel Duffield for all their help and support and for making this book possible. Thanks are also expressed to all the cats photographed with and without their permission, without which this book would not exist.

Bibliography

'The Cat Past and Present', from the French of M Champfleury with supplementary notes by Mrs Cashel Hoey, George Bell and Sons, 1885.
'Domestic and Fancy Cats', John Jennings, L Upcott Gill, c1850-90.
'Our Cats and All About Them', Harrison Weir FRHS, President of the National Cat Club, P Clements and Company, 1889.
'The Book of the Cat', Frances Simpson, Cassell and Company Limited, 1903.
'The Management of Household Pets', 1862.
'Wild Cats of the World', C A W Guggisberg, David and Charles, 1975.
'Wildlife of the Domestic Cat', Roger Tabor, Arrow Books Ltd, 1983.
'The British Museum Book of Cats, Ancient and Modern', Juliet Clutton-Brock, British Museum Publications Ltd, 1985.

Information and journals

'The Cat', Official Journal of the Cats Protection League, 17 Kings Road, Horsham, West Sussex RH13 5PP, England: Group Captain H E Boothby OBE — Editor.
'You And Your Vet' magazine, 7 Mansfield Street, London W1M 0AT, England: Claire Bessant.
'Cat World', 10 West Street, Shoreham-by-Sea, Brighton, West Sussex, England: Joan Moore — Editor.
'Wild About Animals', Kingsgate Business Centre, 12-50 Kingsgate Road, Kingston-Upon-Thames, Surrey KT2 5AA, England: Brenda Marsh — Editor.
'Cats', 5 James Leigh Street, Manchester M1 6EX, England: Brian Poyle — Editor.
'Catfax', 4 Bedford Square, London WC1B 3RA, England: Mary Longhurst. Catfax is a media resource facility and is particularly active in sending out Press Releases and providing a databank of 'cat' information to the media.
'Aristokatt' magazine, Hammerfestgt 2C N-0565, OSLO 5, Norway: Arvid Engh — Norske Rasekattklubbers Riksforbund.
'Cat Fancy' magazine, PO Box 6050, Mission Viejo CA 92690, California, USA: K E Segnar — Managing Editor.
'Cat World International', PO Box 35635, Phoenix, Arizona 85069, USA: Richard and Daphne Negus.
'Pets' magazine, Moorshead Publications Ltd, 1300 Don Mills Road, North York, Toronto, Ontario M3B 3M8, Canada: Marie Hubbs — Editor.
'RAS Cat Control of NSW Journal', Box 4317 — GPO Sydney, New South Wales 2001, Australia: The Editor.

Further reading

'Cat and Kitten Care', David Alderton, Salamander Books Ltd, 1987 (UK).
'Catlopaedia: A complete Guide to Cat Care', J M Evans and Kay White, Henston Limited, 1988 (UK).
'The Cat Care Manual', Bradley Viner, Stanley Paul and Co Ltd, 1987 (UK).
'The Book of the Cat', edited by Michael Wright and Sally Walters, Pan Books Ltd, 1980 (UK).
'An Introduction to Cat Care', Dr Moray Kerv, Apple Press Ltd, 1988 (UK).
'The She Book of Cats', Pamela Carmichael, Ebury Press, 1983 (UK).
'The Observer Book of Cats', Grace Pond, Fredrick Warne, Penguin Books Ltd, 1987 (UK).
'Do Cats Need Shrinks? — Cat Behaviour Explained by a Leading Cat Psychologist and Agony Uncle', Peter Neville, Sidgwick and Jackson, 1990 (UK).
'Catwatching', Desmond Morris, Jonathan Cape, 1986 (UK).
'The Domestic Cat: The Biology of its Behaviour', edited by Dennis C Turner and Patrick Bateson FRS, Cambridge University Press, 1986 (UK).
'A Discovery Guide: The World of Cats', Joan Moore, Salamander Books Ltd, 1989 (UK).
'Understanding Your Cat', Frank Manolson, New Burlington Books, 1984 (UK).
'The Complete Book of Cats', Judith A Steeh, Bison Books Ltd, 1978 (US).
'The Atlas of Cats of the World', Dennis Kelsey-Wood, TFH Publications Inc, 1989 (US).
'American Cat Breeds', Meredith D Wilson, TFH Publications Inc, 1978 (US).

Dedication

To Topaz and Fittleworth and all the glorious felines and their friends everywhere.